THE E[XETER] HAUNTING

by Paul Unwin

SAMUEL FRENCH

THE ENFIELD HAUNTING was first performed at the Theatre Royal, Brighton, on 14 November 2023, followed by performances at Richmond Theatre from 21 November 2023 and then the Ambassadors Theatre, London, from 30 November 2023, presented by MarketStall Productions, The Development Partnership, Smith & Brant Theatricals, Gavin Kalin Productions, Sayers & Sayers Productions Ltd., Eilene Davidson Productions and So Far Productions. The cast was as follows:

PEGGY	Catherine Tate
MAURICE	David Threlfall
JANET	Ella Schrey-Yeats
MARGARET	Grace Molony
JIMMY	Jude Coward Nicoll & Noah Leggott
REY	Mo Sesay
BETTY	Neve McIntosh
WRITER/MAN & Understudy Maurice	Daniel Stewart
OLDER MARGARET & Understudy Peggy/Betty	Stacha Hicks
THE GIRL & Understudy Janet/Margaret	Jasmine Spence
Understudy Rey/Writer/Man	Gareth Radcliffe

Director	Angus Jackson
Set and Costume Designer	Lee Newby
Lighting Designer	Neil Austin
Sound Designer	Carolyn Downing
Illusions Consultant	Paul Kieve
Casting Director	Sophie Holland, CSA
Movement Director	Laura Cubitt
Video Designer	Sam Lisher
Voice & Dialect	Kate Godfrey
Assistant Director	Roberta Zuric

MARKETSTALL

MarketStall is a theatre industry producer and investor, set up in 2023 by John Brant.

The live events arm of The Development Partnership was established in 2021 with the objective of empowering talent and inspiring live story telling in all forms. The company works alongside a range of industry partners in facilitating high-quality events and experiences, including West End and touring theatre shows, concerts and spoken word productions. *The Enfield Haunting* is TDP's maiden West End production.

The Development Partnership sits within The Partnership Group as its production arm; working with the talent and IP represented by this group of agencies and helping bring projects to life across film, TV, theatre and podcasts. The Partnership Group companies include The Artists Partnership, Sayle Screen, Sara Putt Associates, Own it!, Be Heard Voices and TDP.

Producers for The Development Partnership Live Events team are: Roger Charteris, James Beresford and Robert Taylor.

Based in Soho, Smith & Brant Theatricals is independently owned and run by the international and award-winning producers Joseph Smith and John Brant, supported by Fiona Steed. With a background that encompasses the commercial and subsidised sectors, Smith & Brant Theatricals are passionate about developing new work, as well as regularly collaborating on co-productions and offering general management services.

Current projects include: *Cabaret* at The Kit Kat Club (Playhouse Theatre, West End); *Cabaret* (August Wilson Theatre, Broadway); *Plaza Suite* starring Matthew Broderick and two-time Emmy Award-winner Sarah Jessica Parker (Savoy Theatre, West End) and the Tony, Olivier, WhatsOnStage and Critics' Circle Award-winning musical *Come From Away* (UK and Ireland Tour).

Previous Theatre includes: *Come From Away* (Phoenix Theatre in the West End, the Gerald Schoenfeld Theatre in New York, in Toronto, Canada, a North American tour and Comedy Theatre in Melbourne); *Plaza Suite* (The Hudson Theatre, New York); *Fatal Attraction* (UK tour); *Ghost Stories* (Ambassadors Theatre and UK Tour, 2019/20); *Betrayal* starring Tom Hiddleston (Bernard B. Jacobs Theatre, New York, 2019); David Mamet's *Bitter Wheat*, starring John Malkovich (Garrick, 2019); Sam Shepard's *True West*, starring Kit Harington and Johnny Flynn (Vaudeville, 2018/19); Mike Leigh's *Abigail's Party* (UK tour, 2018/19); Patricia Highsmith's *Strangers on a Train*, adapted by Craig Warner and Gaslight, starring Kara Tointon and Keith Allen (UK tours); the Olivier and Tony Award-winning *Memphis: The Musical*, starring Beverley Knight (Shaftesbury, 2014/15); *The Mentalists* by Richard Bean, starring Stephen Merchant (Wyndham's, 2015); *The Pajama Game* (Shaftesbury, 2014); Rob Ashford's hit revival of *How to Succeed in Business Without Really Trying*, starring Daniel Radcliffe (Broadway, 2011/12); *Promises, Promises* (Broadway, 2010); Jonathan Kent's Olivier and Evening Standard Award-winning production of *Sweeney Todd: the Demon Barber of Fleet Street*, starring Michael Ball and Imelda Staunton (West End, 2012).

Producers | Joe Smith and John Brant

General Manager and Associate Producer | Fiona Steed

Production Associate | Laura Sedgwick

Production Assistant | Joshua Vine

GAVIN KALIN PRODUCTIONS

Gavin Kalin Productions is an award-winning theatrical production company that specialise in producing theatre in the West End, on Broadway and internationally.

Recent West End credits include *A Little Life*, *A Streetcar Named Desire*, *Cabaret*, *Back to the Future*, *Cyrano*, *Betrayal*, *9 to 5 The Musical*, *Pretty Woman The Musical*, *Come From Away*, *Pinter at the Pinter*, *Oslo* and *The Ferryman*.

Recent Broadway credits include *A Doll's House*, *Plaza Suite*, *Betrayal*, *Leopoldstadt*, *Funny Girl*, *Sea Wall/A Life* and *The Ferryman*.

Other entertainment: Monopoly Lifesized on Tottenham Court Road, London, now into its third year; the Paddington Bear Experience set to open on the Southbank, London, later this year; and a new permanent immersive theatre with restaurant and bar underneath Waterloo Station named Labyrinth Waterloo.

For more gavinkalinproductions.com

Gavin is also the founder of Totally Theatre Productions Ltd, a TV/Video production company that specialise in producing Broadcast and online content for theatre and live entertainment. Clients are worldwide with many in the West End and on Broadway.

For more totallytheatreproductions.com

SAYERS & SAYERS
PRODUCTIONS

Sayers & Sayers Productions was founded by Michael and Amanda Sayers in 2021 to invest in and produce theatre in the West End.

Current & Previous productions: *The Enfield Haunting* (Ambassadors), *The Pillowman* (Duke of York's) and *The Unfriend* (Criterion).

EILENE DAVIDSON PRODUCTIONS

Current productions include *The Shark is Broken* on Broadway and *The Merchant of Venice* (RSC, tour and London); *A Christmas Carol* (Alexander Palace) and *Macbeth* (UK and US tour).

Recently produced plays on Broadway and in London's West End include the award-winning *Prima Facie* (Harold Pinter Theatre); *A Doll's House* (Playhouse Theatre); *Leopoldstadt* (Wyndham's Theatre) and *Wagatha Christie* (Ambassadors Theatre). In 2022 EDP produced the premiere of Edna O'Brien's *Joyce's Women* (Abbey Theatre, Dublin); the Broadway sensation *Plaza Suite* (Savoy Theatre) and *Anything Goes* (Barbican). Former West End plays include *Uncle Vanya* (Harold Pinter Theatre); *The Grinning Man* and *A Day in the Death of Joe Egg* (Trafalgar Studios); *The Starry Messenger* (Wyndham's Theatre) and the Olivier-winning new play *Emilia* (Vaudeville Theatre).

Eilene formerly worked as an actress and writer in Europe and the USA. Her main interest is in new work, and she was a founder of Stage Traffic, a UK/USA company specialising in producing new plays. She is currently developing new work for production in the UK and USA. She is in the President's Circle at BAFTA and is a member of Society of London Theatre (SOLT) and sits on the Board of the Huntington Theatre in Boston, USA.

Eilene Davidson is an international theatre producer working in the USA, UK and Europe.

PAUL UNWIN, SO FAR PRODUCTIONS, LTD.

Paul is a writer, director and producer. He was Artistic Director of the
Bristol Old Vic where his Associate Directors were Phyllida Lloyd and
Matthew Warchus. For television he was Executive Producer on his
series *Breathless* (ITV/PBS) and is Executive Producer on the German
TV series *Heroes/Berlin*.

CAST

CATHERINE TATE | Peggy

Catherine Tate is an award-winning actor and writer known for her own series *The Catherine Tate Show* and can currently be seen in *Queen Of Oz* for the BBC. She is known to American audiences for playing Nellie Bertram in the US version of The Office on NBC and as Magica De Spell in the Disney reboot of *DuckTales*. Catherine returns as Donna Noble in *Doctor Who* alongside David Tennant's Doctor this year.

Television includes: *Hard Cell* (Netflix), *My First Nativity* (Sky), *Big School* (BBC), *The Bad Mother's Handbook* (Netflix), *Leading Lady Parts* (BBC), *Doctor Who* (BBC), *The Catherine Tate Show*, *Nan's Christmas Carol* and *Catherine Tate's Nan*.

Film includes: *The Nan Movie, Monster Family, SuperBob, Nativity 3, Monte Carlo, Gulliver's Travels, Sixty Six, Starter For Ten*.

Theatre includes: *The Catherine Tate Show Live* (Hammersmith Apollo, West End and International Tour); *Assassins* (The Menier Chocolate Factory); *The Vote* (Donmar Warehouse); *Much Ado About Nothing* (Wyndham's Theatre); *Under The Blue Sky* (The Duke of York's Theatre); *Some Girls* (The Gielgud); *The Exonerated* (Riverside Studios) and *The 24 Hour Plays* (The Old Vic and Broadway). For the National Theatre: *Seasons Greetings, The Way Of The World* and *The Prince's Play*. For the RSC: *A Servant to Two Masters* (West End and International Tour).

DAVID THRELFALL | Maurice

David Threlfall, an RSC Associate Artist who originated the role of Smike in the RSC's acclaimed production of Nicholas Nickleby, was nominated for a Tony Award for his role of Harry in Martin McDonagh's *Hangmen* on Broadway.

Other theatre includes: *Bed of Roses, Someone Who'll Watch Over Me* and *The Rehearsal* for Roundabout; James Duff's *The War At Home, The Traveller, Hamlet, Blue/Orange, Oedipus, The Count of Monte Cristo, Present Laughter, Peer Gynt, Hedda Gabler,* Beckett's *The Old Tune, Faith Healer* and *Don Quixote* for the RSC, directed by Angus Jackson.

His extensive television work includes: Frank Gallagher in the award-winning *Shameless*; *Housewife 49*, written and co-starring Victoria Wood; Sam Beckett in *Waiting for Andre*; *Ripper Street*; *Troy*; *Tommy Cooper*; *The Queen's Sister*; *Conspiracy*; *Paradise Postponed*; Edgar in Laurence Olivier's *King Lear*; *Dodger*; *Funny Woman*; *Passenger*; *Nightsleeper*; *Code Of A Killer* and *The Ark*.

His films include: *Master and Commander, Nowhere Boy, Elizabeth: The Golden Age, Chunky Monkey, Patriot Games, Russia House, Black Sea* and *Hot Fuzz*.

Radio includes: Spike Milligan in *Spike & The Elfin* and Ken Dodd in *Happiness!*

ELLA SCHREY-YEATS | Janet

Television includes: *Secret Invasion, The Witcher, His Dark Materials* and *Silent Witness*.

The Enfield Haunting is Ella's professional stage debut.

Instagram: ella_schrey_yeats

Twitter: ellaschreyyeats

GRACE MOLONY | Margaret

Theatre includes: *The Watsons* (Menier Chocolate Factory and Minerva Theatre, Chichester Festival Theatre); *The Glass Piano* (The Print Room); *Lady Windermere's Fan* (The Vaudeville) and *The Country Girls* (Minerva Theatre, Chichester Festival Theatre).

Television includes: *The Great, Doctors* and *Father Brown.*

Films include: *We Live in Time, Daisy Chain, Artemis Foul, Bone China, Layla, Mary Queen of Scots* and *The Law of Moments.*

Radio includes: *The Country Girls* (BBC Radio 4).

@gracemolony

JUDE COWARD NICOLL | Jimmy

Jude voiced the role of The Boy in the Oscar and BAFTA-winning animation *The Boy, The Mole, The Fox And The Horse* (Bad Robot Productions).

He has appeared at the Traverse Theatre Edinburgh in new plays *Over The Waves, Beneath The Surface* and *Stolen Futures* (Strange Town Youth Theatre).

Television and film includes: forthcoming TV drama *Boat Story, Tom And Jerry, The Lost Sock*, BBC Bitesize online and animation *Bradley And Bee.*

Radio includes: *The Farewell Glacier*, BBC Radio 3 for Naked Productions

The Enfield Haunting is Jude's professional stage debut.

NOAH LEGGOTT | Jimmy

Theatre includes: *Big The Musical* (West End) and *Matilda The Musical* (West End & UK Tour).

Television includes: *A Small Light* and *Crossfire.*

Film includes: *Matilda The Musical, Everybody's Talking about Jamie* and *Juliet, Naked.*

MO SESAY | Rey

Training: Webber Douglas Academy of Dramatic Art.

Theatre includes: Mo has played leading roles at The National, Shakespeare's Globe and more.

Television includes: *Soldier Soldier*, *Dangerfield*, *Murphy's Law*, *Vera* and *Endeavour*, amongst others.

Film includes: *Young Soul Rebels* and *Bhaji on The Beach*.

Mo is also a writer and his TV script about the life of Dr Barnardo has just been optioned by a major television producer.

NEVE McINTOSH | Betty

Theatre includes: *The Scent of Roses* (The Lyceum Edinburgh); *Mouthpiece* (Traverse/ Soho Theatre); *Killer Joe* (Trafalgar Studios); *Meet Me At Dawn* (Traverse Theatre); *The Crucible* (Bristol Old Vic); *The Events* (Edinburgh and New York); *Betrayal* (Citizens Theatre); *The Lady From The Sea* (Royal Exchange Theatre); *Proof* (Perth Theatre); *Three Women* (Edinburgh Fringe); *The Merchant of Venice* (Edinburgh Lyceum); *Great Expectations* (RSC); *The Recruiting Officer* (Lichfield Theatre); *Don Juan* (Sheffield Crucible); *Victoria* (RSC); *Outside On The Street* (The Gate); *Run For Your Wife*, *When We Were Women* (Perth Theatre); *The Trick is To Keep Breathing* (The Tron Theatre) and *The Barber of Seville* (Arches Theatre).

Television includes: *All Creatures Great and Small*, *The Chemistry of Death*, *Shetland*, *Tin Star*, *Stan Lee's Lucky Man*, *Guerilla*, *The Replacement*, *Death in Paradise*, *Critical*, *Ripper Street*, *Dracula*, *Doctor Who*, *Case Histories*, *The Accused*, *Single Father*, *Law & Order: UK*, *Sea Of Souls*, *Low Winter Sun*, *Ghost Squad*, *Miss Marple*, *Bodies*, *Inspector Lynley Mysteries*, *Trial & Retribution*, *The Hound Of The Baskervilles*, *The Fear*, *Lady Audley's Secret*, *Gormenghast*, *Psychos* and *Taggart*.

Film includes: *The Small Hand*, *Social Suicide*, *The Be All and End All*, *Salvage*, *Spring 1941*, *One Last Chance*, *Gypsy Woman*, *The Trouble with Men and Women*, *Plunkett & Macleane* and *The Leading Man*.

Instagram - @nevemcintosh

Twitter - @McIntoshNeve

DANIEL STEWART | Writer/Man/Understudy Maurice

Theatre includes: *Oslo* and *Not About Nightingales* (National Theatre); *Shawshank Redemption* (National Tour); *Written On The Heart*, *Measure For Measure* and *Heresy Of Love* (RSC); *Love Girl And The Innocent* (Southwark Playhouse); *Yonadab* (Chichester Festival Theatre Company); *Country Girl* (The Greenwich Theatre); *The Overwhelming* (The Roundabout Theatre, Broadway); *The Tempest* (The Pittsburgh Public Theatre); *Betrayal* (The Glose Theatre); *Closer* (Portland Centre Stage); *Twelfth Night* and *Around the World in 80 Days* (Cincinnati Playhouse); *Journeys End* and *Witness For The Prosecution* (The Alley Theatre Houston); *Amadeus* and *Beauty Queen Of Leenane* (Syracuse Stage); *Hamlet* and *Twelfth Night* (Shakespeare Theatre of New Jersey) and *Winter's Tale* (Folger Theatre DC).

Television and Film includes: *Blunt Talk, Silent Witness, Summer of Rockets, Law and Order: SVU, SPACE: ABOVE and Beyond, Star Trek: The Next Generation, The Programme, Death Train* and *Servant's Quarters.*

Daniel is also a founding member of Big Space Theatre Company.

@dnstewart67

STACHA HICKS | Older Margaret/Understudy Peggy & Betty

Stacha is an actor, writer, filmmaker and standup comic. She has been part of some brilliant projects in film, theatre and television, in both comedy and drama.

Theatre includes: *My Boys* (Theatre503); *Happy Hour* (Upstairs at the Gatehouse) and *Take me To Manhattan* (Young Vic).

Television and film includes: *Pistol, Captain Phillips, The Children Act, David Brent: Life On The Road, The Owners, Call The Midwife, Holby* and *Casualty.*

As a filmmaker, Stacha writes, directs and produces. Most recently a commission for *Told by An Idiot.* She also directed and co-produced *_ELICIT_* starring Rita Tushingham and Paul Barber, urrently part of the official section for the BAFTA and BIFA qualifying festivals.

JASMINE SPENCE | The Girl/Understudy Janet & Margaret

Training: Italia Conti.

Credits whilst training include: Alice in *Hangmen*, Rachel in *Banana Boys*, Becky in *There Is a War*, and Paulina in *The Winter's Tale.*

Jasmine is thrilled to be making her professional and West End debut in *The Enfield Haunting.*

@jasminespencex

GARETH RADCLIFFE | Understudy Rey and Writer/Man

Gareth is a North Midlander, growing up near Stoke on Trent.

Theatre includes: Bill Sykes in *Oliver Twist* (International tour); Chris in *The Goal* (Hereford Courtyard); Brolls and Parry in *Doctor Who – Time Fracture* (West End); Ted in *War Horse* (UK and International Tour); James in *My Sister Syria* (International Tour); Tony in *Water Under the Bridge* (Brockley Jack); Edmund in *King Lear* and R.P. McMurphy in *One Flew Over the Cuckoo's Nest* (Gaiety Theatre, Isle of Man); Jack in *Life and Death of Martin Luther King* (International Tour); Maurice in *That Catholic Thing* (West End); Jupiter in *The Woman in the Moon* (Rose Bankside Theatre); Dave in *A Hard Days Work* (Southwark Playhouse) and Edgar Allen Poe in *The Mystery of Poe* (International Tour).

He is also a Liverpool FC fan.

CREATIVE

PAUL UNWIN | Writer

Theatre credits include: *Theory For The Attention Of Mr Einstein* (Old Red Lion and Frankfurt); *Doolally Days* (Leicester Haymarket, Tour, Hampstead New End); *This Much Is True – The Killing Of Jean Charles De Menezes*, with Sarah Beck (Theatre503); *At The Point Of Need* (Old Vic) and *The Promise*.

Paul was the Artistic Director of the Bristol Old Vic. His productions there included *In The Ruins* (Bristol Old Vic and Royal Court) and *The Misanthrope* (Bristol Old Vic and National Theatre co-production.)

He worked closely with Arthur Miller on the European premieres of two of his plays: *The Man Who Had All The Luck* and *The Archbishop's Ceiling* (Bristol Old Vic and Young Vic). His other productions included *Hamlet, Othello, Uncle Vanya, The Clandestine Marriage, The Life Of Galileo, The Three Sisters, The Cherry Orchard, Tartuffe, In Times Like These* (by Jeremy Brock) and *The Three Musketeers*. The community play he created, *A Town In The West Country*, involved over three hundred Bristolians and was the subject of a South Bank Show on ITV.

As a freelance director, his productions include *Uncle Vanya* (Gate Theatre Dublin); *Loot* (the Royal Exchange Theatre Manchester) and *The Misanthrope* (Cambridge Theatre.)

Film credits include: His short *Syrup* was nominated for an Oscar and a BAFTA, won the Cannes Jury Prize and the Amnesty International Award. *The American* with Matthew Modine and Diana Rigg (BBC Films); *Elijah* (CTV) won the Gemini and Leo Awards in Canada.

TV directing credits include: *The Bill, Eastenders, Bramwell, NCS, Poirot, Miss Marple, Messiah* and *Casualty*.

He co-created *Breathless* with Peter Grimsdale, directed the first two episodes and wrote the bulk of the series.

He co-created *Casualty* and *Holby City* with Jeremy Brock. *Casualty* is now 37 years old and is the longest-running medical series in the world. To date, the BBC show has won six Royal Television Society awards and six BAFTAs.

Currently, he is working on *58 Seconds* with Jeremy Brock and *Heroes/ Berlin* for German TV.

ANGUS JACKSON | Director

Angus created *Secret Cinema Presents Casino Royale* in London and Shanghai for Secret Cinema in collaboration with EON Productions.

He was the Season Director of the Rome Season for The RSC in Stratford and at The Barbican, directing *Julius Caesar* and *Coriolanus*. Other works directed at the RSC include *Don Quixote* (also Garrick Theatre, West End) and *Oppenheimer* (also Vaudeville Theatre West End).

For the National Theatre he has directed *Rocket to The Moon*, *The Power of Yes*, *Fix Up*, *Elmina's Kitchen* (also Garrick Theatre West End).

As director: *King Lear* (Brooklyn Academy of Music, New York and Chichester Festival Theatre); *Neville's Island* (Chichester Festival Theatre/Duke of York's Theatre West End); Olivier Award-winning *Goodnight Mr Tom* (Duke of York's Theatre and Phoenix Theatre, West End/Children's Touring Partnership); *The Browning Version* (Pinter Theatre, West End and Chichester Festival Theatre) and *Bingo* (Young Vic and Chichester Festival Theatre).

Theatre credits include: *If Only*, *Wallenstein*, *Funny Girl*, *Waltz of the Toreadors*, *The Father*, *Carousel* (Chichester Festival Theatre); *The Prayer Room* (Edinburgh Festival and Birmingham Rep); *Promises Promises*, *Sexual Perversity In Chicago* (Crucible Theatre Sheffield); *24 Hour Plays* (American Airlines Theatre Broadway/Old Vic) and *Drink Dance Laugh and Lie* (Bush Theatre).

As adapter: *The Boy In The Striped Pyjamas* (No 1 tour for Children's Touring Partnership), and Angus is currently adapting a novel for the RSC.

Films credits include: *Epithet*, *Running For River*, *Old Street*, *Elmina's Kitchen* for which he was nominated for the Best New Director BAFTA.

LEE NEWBY | Set and Costume Designer

Theatre includes: *I'm Sorry Prime Minister* (Bath Theatre Royal); *The Last Five Years* (Garrick Theatre/China Tour); *Labour of Love* (Noël Coward Theatre); *The Life I Lead* (Wyndham's Theatre/UK Tour); Ian McKellen's *Hamlet* and *The Cherry Orchard* (Theatre Royal Windsor); *Steve* (Seven Dials Playhouse); *Wodehouse In Wonderland* (UK Tour); *Les Misérables* (The Mack Theatre); *My Night with Reg* (Turbine Theatre); *Killing The Cat* (Riverside Studios); *Romeo and Juliet* and *Richard III* (Shakespeare's Rose Theatre, York); *Homos* and *Or Everyone in America* (Finborough Theatre); *MUSIK* (Leicester Square Theatre); *Vienna 1934–Munich 1938* (Ustinov Studio Theatre, Bath); *The View Upstairs* (Soho Theatre); *The Importance of Being Earnest* (Theatr Clwyd); *Abigail's Party* (UK Tour); *SUS*, *Mother of Him*, *Whodunnit [Unrehearsed]* and

Gently Down the Stream (Park Theatre); *The Last Five Years, Grand Hotel* and *Dogfight* (Southwark Playhouse); *Mythic* (Charing Cross Theatre); *Lunch* and *The Bow of Ulysses* (Trafalgar Studios); *Floyd Collins* (Wilton's Music Hall); *A Prayer for Wings and Jerker* (King's Head Theatre); *Spin, MUSIK, The Crown – Live!* and *Cruel Intentions* (Edinburgh Festival); *The Tempest, Deathwatch* and *Ignis* (Coronet Theatre).

NEIL AUSTIN | Lighting Designer

West End theatre includes: *Medea* (Soho Theatre); *Frozen* (Theatre Royal Drury Lane); *Harry Potter and the Cursed Child* (Palace); *Leopoldstadt, The Starry Messenger, Red, The Weir, Hamlet, Madame de Sade, Twelfth Night* (Wyndham's); *Company, Frost/Nixon* (Gielgud); *Rosmersholm, Ink, No Man's Land* (Duke of York's); *The Night of the Iguana, The Lieutenant of Inishmore, Labour of Love, Photograph 51, Shakespeare in Love, Henry V* (Coward); *The Goat, Great Britain* (Haymarket); *Travesties, A Life in the Theatre* (Apollo); *Buried Child, The Hothouse, Dealer's Choice* (Trafalgar Studios); *The Sunshine Boys* (Savoy); *South Downs, The Browning Version, Death and the Maiden, The Children's Hour* (Comedy/Pinter); *Piaf, The Prisoner of Second Avenue* (Vaudeville); *King Lear, The Seagull* (RSC: New London); *Bend it Like Beckham* (Phoenix); *Betty Blue Eyes* and *Much Ado About Nothing* (Novello).

Other theatre includes: *The 47th* (Old Vic), *Tammy Faye: The Musical, The Hunt, Albion, Ink, The Treatment* and *Medea* (Almeida); *After Life, Translations, Three Days in the Country, Rules for Living, Dara, Liolà, Children of the Sun, The Cherry Orchard, Women Beware Women, London Assurance, The White Guard, Oedipus, Philistines, The Man of Mode* and *Thérèse Raquin* (National Theatre); *Henry IV, Julius Caesar, The Night Alive, Spelling Bee, King Lear, Passion, The Wild Duck, After Miss Julie* and *Caligula* (Donmar Warehouse).

Broadway includes: *Leopoldstadt, Company, Harry Potter and the Cursed Child, Ink, Travesties, Hughie, Cat on a Hot Tin Roof, Evita, Red, Hamlet, The Seafarer, Frost/Nixon.*

Awards include: 2019 Tony Award for *Ink*; 2019 Helpmann Award, 2018 Tony, Drama Desk, Outer Critics Circle and 2017 Olivier and WhatsOnStage Awards for *Harry Potter and the Cursed Child*; 2019 Knight of Illumination award for *Company*; 2011 Laurence Olivier Award for *The White Guard*, and the 2010 Tony and Drama Desk awards for *Red*.

CAROLYN DOWNING | Sound Designer

Carolyn Downing is a Tony and Olivier award-winning sound designer working in a variety of fields including exhibitions, fashion, theatre and live events. Creativity and collaboration are at the heart of her work from initial concept development with fellow designers through to realisation with technical and project delivery teams.

Theatre and live events includes: *Commonwealth Games Opening Ceremony* (Birmingham Alexander Stadium, 2022); *Life Of Pi* (West End, Boston A.R.T & Broadway – NY Times Critics Pick, winner of Tony Award for Best Sound Design 2023, nominated for Olivier Award for Best Sound Design 2021 and awarded UK Theatre Award for Best Design 2019); *Fatal Attraction* (UK Tour, 2022); *Fantastically Great Women* (UK Tour, 2021); *Summer & Smoke* (Almeida theatre, nominated for Olivier Award for Best Sound Design 2019); *A Number* (The Bridge Theatre); *The Normal Heart* (2021), *The Welkin* (2020), *Downstate* (also at Steppenwolf Chicago 2018/19), *Mr Gum & The Dancing Bear – The Musical* (2019), *As You Like It* (2015), *Our Country's Good* (2015), *The Motherf***er With The Hat* (2015), *Dara* (2015), *Protest Song* (2012) and *Double Feature* (2011) (National Theatre); *Death Of A Salesman* (Young Vic/WE, 2019/20); *All My Sons* (Old Vic, 2019); *White Teeth* (Kiln Theatre, 2018); *Gypsy* (2019), *The Producers* (2018) (The Royal Exchange Theatre, Manchester); *Chimerica* (Almeida Theatre/West End, awarded Olivier for Best Sound Design 2014); *Carmen Disruption* (2015), *Blood Wedding* (2006) (Almeida Theatre); *Me And My Girl* (2018), *Fiddler On The Roof* (2017) (Chichester Festival Theatre); *BLANK* (2019), *Les Liaisons Dangereusse* (also on Broadway 2015/16), *Fathers and Sons* (2014), *Lower Ninth* (2010), *Dimetos* (2009) and *Absurdia* (2008) (Donmar Warehouse); *Hope* (2014), *The Low Road* (2013) and *Choir Boy* (2012) (Royal Court); *Fantastic Follies Of Mrs Rich* (2017), *Julius Caesar* (2017), *Anthony & Cleopatra* (2017), *Coriolanus* (2017), *The Gods Weep* (2010), *The Winter's Tale* (2007) and *Pericles* (2007) (RSC); *The Believers* (2014), *Beautiful Burnout* (2010) and *Love Song* (2011) (Frantic Assembly).

Designs for opera include: *Benjamin De Derniere Nuit* (Opera De Lyon, 2016); *How the Whale Became* (Royal Opera House, 2013); *American Lulu* (Opera Group, 2013); and *After Dido* (ENO, 2009).

Her work in exhibitions spans a variety of styles and venues including *Jean-Michel Basquiat: King Pleasure* (NYC and World Tour, 2022–ongoing); *Reimagining Wordsworth* (The Wordsworth Trust, Grasmere, 2020); *Hut 11A: The Bombe Breakthrough* (Bletchley Park, 2018); *Mary Quant* (2019) and *So You Say You Want A Revolution? Records & Rebels*

1965-70 (2016) (V&A); *Exhibitionism: The Rolling Stones* (Saatchi Gallery, 2016); *Louis Vuitton: Series 3* (2015); *Collider* (2014) and *The Constellation Storybox* (2015) (Science Museum); and *From Street to Trench* (Imperial War Museum North, 2014).

Carolyn has created soundscapes for *Shawn Mendes Illuminate Tour 2017* and *Louis Vuitton: Spring/Summer 2015, Fall 2015, Spring/Summer 2016, Spring/Summer 2017 Ready To Wear Collection* shows at The Louis Vuitton Foundation & The Louvre, Paris. Carolyn has also co-created a geo-located audio experience as part of The Estuary Festival 2021 called *Ness* by Robert Macfarlane, developed with director Zoe Svendsen.

For further information and updates – www.carolyndowning.co.uk

PAUL KIEVE | Illusions Consultant

RSC: *Matilda The Musical, Julius Caesar, The Winter's Tale, The Cherry Orchard, The Tempest, Alice in Wonderland, Dr Jekyll and Mr Hyde, The Mysteries, Spring Awakening, Arabian Nights, The Tempest.* Paul has created original magic for over 100 live productions around the world.

Theatre includes: *Groundhog Day* (Old Vic/Broadway); *Theatre of Blood, La Grande Magia, Her Naked Skin* (National Theatre); *Ghost the Musical* (Broadway Drama Desk Award), *Pippin, Side Show, An Act of God* (Broadway); *Roald Dahl's The Witches, The Invisible Man, The Lord of the Rings, Zorro* (West End); *Macbeth* (MIF); *L'Heure Espagnole* (ROH); *Alice in Wonderland* (Royal Ballet/English National Ballet); *Mary Poppins* (West End) and *Instructions for Correct Assembly* (Royal Court).

Television includes: *Cranford, Saturday Night Takeaway, Heroes of Magic.*

Film includes: *Wonka* (2023), *Harry Potter and the Prisoner of Azkaban, Hugo.*

Books: *Hocus Pocus* (Bloomsbury), published in 11 languages.

Other: *Catherine Tate Live, Mickey and the Magician* (Disneyland Paris); *Before The Dawn* (Kate Bush), *Adele* (Las Vegas) and *Awakening at Wynn, Las Vegas.*

He has consulted with magicians including Derren Brown, Penn and Teller, David Copperfield, Dynamo and David Blaine. A Gold Star Member of the Inner Magic Circle and recipient of their Maskelyne award (services to British magic) and the Creative Fellowship of the Academy of Magical Arts (Magic Castle) Hollywood. www.stageillusion.com

SOPHIE HOLLAND, CSA | Casting Director

Sophie Holland is the Casting Director for epic TV franchise *The Witcher*: Netflix's first International Original series.

Additional projects include: *Constellations* (Apple TV), *THE PERIPHERAL* (Amazon), *The Continental* (John Wick Prequel for STARZ/Lionsgate), *Knuckles* (Paramount), Tim Burton's *Wednesday* (Netflix), *Vampire Academy* for NBC, Season 4 of Netflix's acclaimed series of *YOU* and season 2 of *Shadow And Bone* (Netflix/21 Laps).

Film includes: Sophie is the Casting Director for the highly anticipated Tim Burton film *Beetlejuice 2* (Warner Bros), *SONIC 3* (Paramount) and UK casting for *Mission Impossible 8: Dead Reckoning Part 2* (Paramount), *Back In Action* (Netflix) and *Cherry* (AGBO Films/Apple TV). Casting on A24's *The Kill Team* with Alexander Skarsgård and a modern retelling of Wolfgang Amadeus Mozart's popular opera *The Magic Flute*.

Theatre includes: *Against* (Almeida) and *Hamlet* (Young Vic). Sophie was also Casting Director for the Almeida's *Greek* season including most notably *The Iliad* casting over 50 of the UK's most well-known actors for a 24 hour reading of Homer's epic tale.

LAURA CUBITT | Movement Director

As director: *Dragons and Mythical Beasts* (Regent's Park Open Air Theatre & Tour).

As puppetry director: *Romeo and Juliet* (NT Puppetry Consultant); *Pinocchio* (The Unicorn); *Macbeth* (Red Rose Chain); *A Monster Calls* (Chichester Festival Theatre & tour); *The Boy in the Dress* (RSC); *The Little Prince* (Fuel); *Don Quixote* (RSC Puppetry Co-Director); *A Monster Calls* (The Old Vic/Bristol Old Vic); *Small Island* (NT); *Common* (NT); *Dinosaur World Live* (UK/US tour); *Rudolph* (Birmingham Mac); *The Curious Incident of the Dog in the Night-Time* (NT/West End Puppetry Consultancy); *Brilliant* (Fevered Sleep Puppetry Consultant); *Running Wild* (Chichester Festival Theatre/UK Tour Associate Puppetry Director); *Goodnight Mr Tom* (West End/UK Tour Associate Puppetry Director).

As movement director: *Pinocchio* (The Unicorn); *Run Sister Run* (Paines Plough/Soho Theatre/Sheffield Theatres); *Anna* (NT Associate Movement Director); *Oppenheimer* (RSC/West End Movement Re-Staging); *War Horse* (NT Berlin Associate Movement Director); *2012 Olympics Opening* (Associate Movement Director).

As performer: *Peter Pan, Elephantom, Women Beware Women, War Horse* (NT); *Oppenheimer, Shoemakers Holiday* (RSC); *The Lorax* (The Old Vic); *Faeries* (Royal Opera House); *State of the Union* (BBC 2).

KATE GODFREY | Voice & Dialect

Having worked as an actor for ten years, Kate trained as a voice coach at The Central School of Speech and Drama in 1995–96. Her first job was at Mountview Theatre School and then The Guildhall School of Music and Drama. Whilst freelancing in the West End, she was also part of the National Theatre's voice department for 18 years. She left both The National and Guildhall in 2015 to become Head of Voice at the RSC until 2020. Her most recent work has been voice coach to Jodie Comer on *Prima Facie* (West End and New York); *Village Idiot* (Theatre Royal Stratford East); *Ocean at the End of the Lane* (West End and UK Tour) and The National Theatre's transfer to the Gielgud Theatre of *The Crucible*.

ROBERTA ZURIC | Assistant Director

Roberta is a freelance theatre director and facilitator.

Directing credits include: *Reset The Stage* (The Mono Box/Apatan Productions); *No Planet B* (Cut the Cord/Jackson's Lane); *The Burning* (Pleasance, Edinburgh); *The Wave* (Almeida); *All Quiet on the Western Front* (Pleasance, SoHo Playhouse, NYC); *Alice in the Cuckoo's Nest* (Librarian Theatre/UK Tour); *Zero for the Young Dudes!* (Orange Tree Theatre/Albany/National Theatre) and *Thisbe* (Door Ajar Theatre National Tour).

She has assisted on productions at the RSC, Shakespeare's Globe, Arcola, Nevill Holt Opera and National Opera Studio.

Alongside directing, Roberta is an associate artist of National Youth Theatre, and Education Associate at The Old Vic.

WHERE IT BEGAN by Paul Unwin

It was my agent's husband's idea. Jeremy Thomas had read about 'The Enfield Haunting' and thought it would make an exciting play.

Dutiful, a few weeks later, I went to meet Guy Lyon Playfair in his flat in Earl's Court. The story he told, and how he told it, was fascinating and unsettling.

That chilly September afternoon was nearly eleven years ago. Guy was in his mid-seventies, and there was something intense and melancholic about him. He spoke quietly and carefully about the years – more than half his life – he had spent tracking down, writing about, and trying to understand paranormal and poltergeist events.

He had lived in South America and in India and had witnessed some extraordinary things. He wasn't present when a thirteen-year-old girl in Brazil was burnt to death but arrived soon after. He did witness a family chased out of their home when roof tiles were flung at them… but nothing, he suggested, was as extraordinary and sustained as what happened to a working-class single mother and her children in Enfield in the late 1970s.

As the afternoon darkened, Guy took boxes of tapes from a shelf in his living room and started to play recordings he and Maurice Grosse had made.

A twelve-year-old girl, Janet Hodgson, appears to have been at the centre of what unfolded during 1977 and 1978. The recordings were of her 'speaking'. As soon as Guy pressed play, I knew that the voice on the tape could not easily come from a young girl but I was uneasy. Some of the things she said were, frankly, silly. Sometimes, the voice was rude – scatological – and when asked who was speaking, the voice spelt out: G-H-O-S- T. It felt childish, and the voice was saying things that a young child might say if they were *pretending* to be a ghost.

However, as Guy played more recordings, the mood changed. Sometimes, the voice seemed to be howling in pain. I asked Guy to stop the tape. I needed to catch my breath. How did he reconcile the childish words with this much more troubling voice? He answered my question with his own. How could young Janet even make these voices? He asked me to imitate her – in less than a minute, I had a sore throat and couldn't go on.

He played more tapes. It was late afternoon by now. Guy was reserved but sensitive. He had faced sceptics all his career and got quite angry over tea and biscuits, complaining how easy scepticism was and how complex these cases were. The logic puzzle frustrated him: he knew the contradiction. How could a child make these voices, and yet why would they say such childish things? How could objects be thrown around the house, and a young girl flung from her bed, when at other times it was clear one of the children had thrown something, and Janet and her sister Margaret admitted they had faked some of the events? Surely, he asked with a weary smile, poltergeists could at least be consistent.

Guy's collaborator and friend, Maurice Grosse, had died a few years earlier. Guy described this kind, thorough and careful man with deep affection. He greatly respected him – and it was clear he helped the family enormously. Maurice was always reassuring and spent a huge amount of time at 284 Green Street, sleeping downstairs, waiting to intervene if things 'kicked off'. Even Guy admitted that when he threatened to overwhelm the small house with paranormal experts, Maurice tried to resist. He was determined to protect an already strung-out and exhausted family.

Guy talked a lot about the children's mother. Peggy was a single parent and a lioness protecting her children, but the family was very poor and, significantly, never asked for money or profited in any way from what they were going through. The strain Peggy must have been under, Guy said, was almost overwhelming.

It was night and chilly outside when Guy told me how Maurice had lost his daughter in an accident, and that he never let the family know that he was grieving himself.

Five hours after I arrived, I had to go. I thanked Guy, but in his stairwell, he carefully asked if I believed what he had described. I didn't know.

Walking through the crowds to the underground in the rain, I suddenly felt surprisingly emotional. Everyone who passed me, huddled against the cold, were living their lives. Some were happy, some were sad. But all individuals – all with their own realities. I started to think about the relationship between what we all assume we *understand* and the many things that simply confound us. I wondered how our strange human brains could become so easily convinced of things that are untrue but couldn't get Hamlet out of my head: "There are more things in heaven and earth, Horatio, / Than are dreamt of in our philosophy."

The more I thought about what Guy had told me about what had happened to this 'ordinary' working-class family in Enfield, the stranger and more startling it seemed to become. This wasn't about ghosts in old vicarages or country estates. This was something weird and shocking in a normal home, on a normal street, in Enfield.

I began to wonder if it had something to do with forces being unleashed. Extreme emotions may have triggered behaviour, but I also knew behaviour-triggering emotions can have shocking consequences. Did the persistence of what happened in Enfield and its violence suggest something terribly powerful was going on in that small house on Green Street? Could emotions be so extreme that something else 'happened'? Or was there something in the house – some force – that needed a vessel to express itself?

THE ENFIELD HAUNTING is my attempt to understand. Although the play is inspired by real events and by real people, it is in no way a documentary. Many of the events we show happened, and the key characters are based on real people, but theatre is a place to imagine... Imagine what happens when we face the extraordinary.

CHARACTERS

WRITER – a middle-class voice on a telephone.

OLDER MARGARET – a voice on the telephone.

PEGGY – Late forties. Working class, deep feeling, a lioness under a nervy shell.

REY – Late forties. Working class. Never left home, now lives alone with his cat.

JIMMY – Twelve. Very intense. Bad stutter.

MARGARET – Seventeen. Bursting with pubescent energy.

JANET – Sixteen. Gaunt, bags under her eyes, intense in a haunted girl kind of way.

MAURICE – Mid-sixties. An upper-middle-class man. He is tender and warm. He wears a moustache, bow ties, etc.

THE MAN

THE GIRL

BETTY – mid-fifties, Maurice's wife. Dignified in her grief.

AUTHOR'S NOTES

The play can be performed by eight actors with **WRITER/MAN**, **JANET/GIRL** and **BETTY/OLDER MARGARET** doubling.

No interval.

THE ENFIELD HAUNTING is inspired by real events and by real people. Much of what we show happened, and some characters are based on real people. However, it is a play and does not profess to be a true re-enactment of the events surrounding this notorious and extraordinary story. It is a work of imagination.

Scene One

(Snap blackout – A mobile phone chirps...and chirps...and chirps. Maybe we start to laugh. Then, finally, it is answered. Two voices in the darkness.)

OLDER MARGARET. 'ello?

(Her voice has a rasp – from a thousand cigarettes.)

WRITER. Oh, hi there – is that Margaret? Margaret Hodgson?

OLDER MARGARET. Who is this?

*(**WRITER** is middle class, upbeat, breezy. **OLDER MARGARET** is flinty, taut.)*

WRITER. I know it's all a really long time ago but they said you might be prepared to talk?

OLDER MARGARET. How did you get my number?

WRITER. There's so much stuff on YouTube and on the net and I'm sure most of it is absolute rubbish. I want to...

OLDER MARGARET. How d'you get this number? I don't like people having this...

WRITER. Please, Margaret listen to me. All I want is to know the truth.

*(Silence. Just **OLDER MARGARET** breathing.)*

Hey, why don't I come down? I can meet you somewhere? A cafe? Near the station... Or on the beach? For a walk?

OLDER MARGARET. Please. I don't want to talk to no journalists. It's all been said.

WRITER. I'm not a journalist.

OLDER MARGARET. Now please...

WRITER. Can I talk to Janet then?

> *(Silence. Finally...)*

OLDER MARGARET. No.

WRITER. I know what happened to Jimmy...

OLDER MARGARET. You don't!

WRITER. I know what I have been told. And what I've read.

Where is Janet? Has she passed...?

OLDER MARGARET. She went through enough.

WRITER. Can't I speak with her? We need – I need – to know the truth.

OLDER MARGARET. Leave it alone.

WRITER. *It?* What do you mean?

> *(Silence from* **OLDER MARGARET** *– just maybe a breath.)*

Please.

> *(Lights build, revealing the skeletal shadows of a set.)*

What do you mean by 'it'?

Scene Two

(Imagine you had ripped a house in half. The house is a study in 1978.)

(284 Green Street, Enfield, was built between the wars. It hasn't been redecorated for years. The poverty is visceral.)

(There is a Formica kitchen off a living area. The living area has a TV, a built-in gas fire, sofa, armchair and table.)

(Upstage centre – at the end of the downstairs hall – the front door. There is a toilet off the hall. Off to one side is a staircase to the bedroom. The bedroom has several beds crammed into it, flock wallpaper, and a thin curtain over a window. 1970s posters cover one wall.)

*(Downstairs, **PEGGY** is sat at the table. She has a needle and thread and is re-repairing a piece of one of her children's clothing: a pair of pyjama bottoms. **PEGGY** is in her mid-forties but looks older. She is a lioness with deeply rattled nerves. But now she is happily humming to herself. A moment.)*

(Upstage, the front door opens – we just catch a shadow.)

PEGGY. *(Without turning, calling.)* You're back early!

*(**PEGGY** goes on stitching. Suddenly, a large man in a boiler suit looms over her.)*

REY. *(Cod ghost.)* Whooah, whooah!

*(**PEGGY** screams, he laughs.)*

I surprised you!

(**PEGGY** *is furious but laughs nervously. A
big part of her is trying to remain positive at
all times.*)

PEGGY. Dear God, Rey you near gave me a heart attack.
You gave me a fright, you did. What are you doin'
creeping in like that?

(**REY** *is a big man. Uncomfortable in himself
but kind.*)

REY. You gave me the keys, when they took you to the
seaside. You remember!

PEGGY. Not so you can creep in like that!

REY. Thought I'd see how you were...

(**REY** *holds out a box of Quality Street sweets.
This is an important moment for* **REY**.*)*

PEGGY. What the heavens?

REY. I bought them for you, Peggy.

PEGGY. For me...?

REY. I'm worried about you.

PEGGY. There's nothing to worry about!

(**REY** *looks around – and whispers.*)

REY. They here? His Jaguar's not out there. Quite a motor
that, I can tell you. That is not going to be cheap to run,
not with the Sheiks taking their pound of flesh.

PEGGY. The children will be home any second now.

REY. I know. That's why I wanted to see you. And give you
them.

(*He carefully puts the sweets on the table, but he
doesn't know what to do next. There's a pause.*)

PEGGY. Well. There. I have my nippers' dinner to make, Rey.

(She stands and goes upstage to the kitchen. **REY** *hovers.)*

REY. At least the rain has held off. They say it's going to be a scorcher. The weekend.

(He looks around, checks that **PEGGY**'s *back is turned in the kitchen and goes across to the armchair.* **REY** *looks at it. Steps away from it. He then drops into a squat and lifts the heavy chair so he can look underneath. Upstage – beyond the kitchen window – a loud miaow and a glimpse of a black cat.* **PEGGY** *turns, watches* **REY** *–)*

PEGGY. What are you doing?

REY. Nothing!

(Startled, he drops the chair and straightens.)

Wanted to get to the bottom of things, Peggy.

PEGGY. *(Changing the subject.)* You should feed that poor cat, sometimes, you know. Spider's in and out of our garden, hungry like she's starvin' to death...

REY. I do, but I can't control her.

PEGGY. She's possessed – that's what Mr Playfair reckons!

(She laughs and turns back to the kitchen.)

REY. Listen to me, please, Peggy.

PEGGY. What did you want Rey? Because if it's to give me a talking to, I'm not sure I'm interested.

(And she turns to go back to the kitchen. **REY** *clears his throat – this is his moment.)*

REY. I... we... think it's got to stop.

PEGGY. What has got to stop?

REY. What is going on! Here. Something bad is going to happen.

> (**PEGGY** *returns to lay the table. She puts her needlework and repaired clothing carefully on the sideboard.*)

People are talking.

PEGGY. Well we *were* in the newspaper. On the front page.

REY. And on the TV. On the BBC!

(Smiling.) You've certainly put Green Street, Enfield, on the map! We all...

PEGGY. *(Interrupting.)* It's got nothing to do with anyone, Rey.

REY. I... we...

PEGGY. Who's this 'we', when they are at home?

REY. The Police.

PEGGY. *(Alarmed.)* What have you said to the Police?!

REY. No what I mean, even them, comin' here!

> (**PEGGY** *stares at him.*)

Your girls – I don't know much about these things – but they are a pair of minxes. You know that. Young girls can get up to all sorts...

PEGGY. You're right. You don't know much about young girls.

REY. No, but I am trying to help.

(Trying again.) You know me, Peggy, I don't want trouble. I was born next door. This is where I live. I see the comings and the goings. I seen them. All of them.

(Declaration.) If it's anything, and I don't think it is anything, myself, it's that chair.

PEGGY. I have no idea what's got into you.

REY. I see how tired you all are, and I just want to help.

PEGGY. *(Wanting none of this.)* Thank you for the Quality Street. My favourite. I'll put them away for a rainy day.

> *(The front door opens with a bang, and* **JIMMY** *[eleven, strange, with a terrible stutter] flies in. His school uniform is darned and re-darned. Without stopping, he lands in front of the TV – puts it on – JIMMY SAVILE'S JIM'LL FIX IT. He doesn't take his eyes off the screen as he talks.)*

JIMMY. I h-h-ate them.

PEGGY. Jimmy, darlin', who now...?

> *(She is crossing to* **JIMMY** *when* **MARGARET** *[seventeen – in a tight tank top and tighter loon pants – bursting with pubescent sexual energy] comes in from the front door.)*

MARGARET. Why'd you run away like that Jimmy yer little tit?

PEGGY. Oh dear what happened?

JIMMY. N-n-othing.

MARGARET. Some of the boys said we was a bunch of liars and J-J-J-immy just ran away when he could've stood an' fought like a fuckin' man.

REY. You might want to watch your language, young lady.

MARGARET. And you might want to shut your gob, Uncle Rey.

> *(Then,* **MARGARET** *laughs uproariously.* **MARGARET** *has a strange energy. She never settles and her laugh, and her movement, feels uneasy.)*

REY. Margaret, I'll not have anyone speak to me like that.

PEGGY. *(To* **JIMMY.***)* They don't know what they are talking about. Come on, Jimmy, my love.

> *(She scrunches his hair but* **JIMMY** *leans in and whacks up the TV volume, his face is inches from the screen. It's now very loud.)*

MARGARET. Well, will you look at these!

> *(She has the Quality Streets,* **PEGGY** *takes them.)*

PEGGY. For a rainy day.

MARGARET. *(Smiling.)* From Uncle Rey? Cheeky monkey. He's a right flirt, mum.

  (To **REY.***)* You're a right flirt aren't you?

PEGGY. Where's Jan'?

MARGARET. Last seen floating six feet in the air in the middle of the playground...

> *(Her laugh, again.)*

PEGGY. I wish you'd look after Janet, I really do.

> *(***PEGGY** *runs fast out the front door.* **JIMMY** *takes a chair from the table and puts it in front of the TV. He then sits on it, his legs scrunched up.* **MARGARET** *stalks. She goes up to the kitchen, gets a glass of water, and appears through the hatch. She smiles warmly.)*

MARGARET. You staying for tea, Rey? Be fish fingers.

REY. Oh no just wanted to have a word with you. You two young ladies, particularly.

  (To **JIMMY** *– who is only inches from the TV.)* You want to turn that thing off son?

(**JIMMY** *doesn't react.*) Jimmy, lad, please.

> (**REY** *now moves to the TV and is about to switch it off. But* **MARGARET** *has moved like lightning and is suddenly half an inch from* **REY***'s face.*)

MARGARET. You touch that an' we'll do you from the inside out.

REY. *(Frightened.)* You don't frighten me Margaret.

> (*Then* **JANET** *appears at the front door. She wears a school uniform and carries a satchel. She is sixteen, blonde, with sallow grey skin. Dark rings under her eyes. She is extraordinary: fragile, but also very powerful. She stops. Stares at* **REY**. *For a moment, he doesn't know what to say – the stare is uncomfortable.*)

There she is! Your poor mum is worried sick, Janet.

> (**JANET** *walks straight to the table and pulls an exercise book from her satchel. She sits, takes out a school book and locks into her homework, writing fast with a pencil.* **PEGGY** *comes from the front door, following.*)

You found her! That's good, isn't it?

PEGGY. *(Bright.)* Who's hungry? Who wants their din-dins?

> (*None of the* **CHILDREN** *respond.* **PEGGY** *goes upstage to the kitchen.*)

REY. Hard to hear yourself think with that on... *(The TV.)*

> (**REY** *is in the middle of the room.* **JIMMY** *is half an inch from the TV screen,* **PEGGY** *upstage,* **MARGARET** *turns, goes.*)

MARGARET. *(Indicating the loo corridor.)* Pardonnez moi.

> *(She walks towards* **REY** *and passes him provocatively close.)*

You be good Uncle Rey, when I am not here to keep an eye on you.

> *(She goes. The TV is really loud.)*

REY. *(Uneasy.)* Anything I can do, Mrs Hodgson?

> *(***PEGGY*** *is in the kitchen – making tea.* **REY** *drifts over – looks over* **JANET***'s shoulder. She blocks his view of what she is writing. He hesitates and then...)*

I was never much use when it came to school. Tricky, Jan'?

> *(Silence but for Jimmy Savile on the TV.)*

You gave Mrs Washington a right fright. Says she saw you from across the zebra crossing flying – or something – in the upstairs front.

> *(***JANET*** *hunches intensely.)*

You look like you haven't had a night's sleep. Janet, I've known you for, well, it must be five years since you moved in here. You were such a lovely little thing – skipping and playing...

> *(***PEGGY*** *has appeared from the kitchen. She is carrying a teapot. She stops.)*

PEGGY. Rey I want you to stop. I want you to go. What is happening here is nothing to do with you.

REY. But nothing is happening! The kids are just running rings...

(And then there's a very loud bang. REY spins, but PEGGY doesn't even appear to notice and puts the teapot on the table.)

PEGGY. *(Quietly, tenderly.)* Jan', dear, you want to put that homework to one side so you can eat. There's a good girl.

> *(But JANET doesn't stop her intense writing as REY announces:)*

REY. You got an air-block in your plumbing Peggy, I'd reckon. That's all that it is!

PEGGY. Jimmy, please...

JIMMY. I-I-I want to see this.

> *(There's another very loud bang. PEGGY goes back to the kitchen.)*

REY. *(Excited.)* That's Margaret! She's the minx bangin' like that!

(Calling, laughing.) Margaret stop that banging will you?

> *(The table JANET is sitting at suddenly thumps loudly. REY spins to look at JANET. She's still scribbling away. Then the TV dies.)*

JIMMY. Fer f-ucks sake Jan'! Not the f-uckin' TV!

REY. Language! Jimmy...

> *(The table is starting to shake. JANET stops her writing and stares ahead. REY looks at her and then grabs the teapot. JIMMY is thumping the TV to make it work. MARGARET saunters back from the downstairs toilet and goes upstairs...)*

JIMMY. *(Shouting.)* Jan' you do this?!

*(Suddenly, **JANET**'s eyes roll into her head, and she starts to shake and stare upwards.)*

*(Upstairs in the bedroom, **MARGARET** plops the needle on a little Dansette record player. The Bay City Rollers' "I Only Want to Be With You" blasts out.)*

*(**REY** is holding the teapot.)*

REY. *(Shocked.)* Janet – you alright, dear? Is she alright?

*(**PEGGY** is in the kitchen, getting on with the kids' dinner. **JIMMY** is thumping the TV to make it work.)*

JIMMY. You k-know h-ow to fix this Un-cle Rey?

*(Upstairs, **MARGARET** is dancing around to the music. It is weird because as the music gets louder, she seems to be throwing herself against the walls of the small room.)*

*(Downstairs, the table shaking is becoming very powerful. And then **JANET** starts making a weird grumbling noise.)*

REY. Oh now come on Janet! Mrs H… She's making this up. You're making this up!

JANET. Grrehhhhhh. Grrrrrrrr.

*(**MARGARET** is upstairs singing along with the Bay City Rollers, she's loud, excited.)*

REY. Janet – stop that. Girl, you got to stop that!

*(**JIMMY** has now crawled behind the TV and has the plug out. **MARGARET** is singing and dancing upstairs. **JANET** is growling… The table is shaking horribly. **PEGGY**, however, is calmly preparing the food.)*

*(Suddenly, **JANET** screams at the top of her lungs, and the table is still. The record player stops at the top of the scream. **MARGARET** slumps onto a bed. **JIMMY** freezes. Silence.)*

PEGGY. Them Bay City Rollers will have my sanity to answer for.

*(**JANET** is hunched over.)*

JANET. *(Sobbing, absolutely real.)* Uncle Rey stabbed me!

*(**REY** is holding one of **PEGGY**'s sewing needles. **PEGGY** stands upstage holding two plates of fish fingers.)*

REY. Just a little prick! Just wanted to see if she was faking!

*(**JANET** turns to **REY**.)*

JANET. He stabbed me, mum.

PEGGY. Rey you have to go!

REY. *(Shaken.)* Peggy I just wanted to see if she's making this all up.

*(To **JANET**.)* I didn't mean any harm. It's all make-believe, isn't it?

*(Then **JANET** snaps back into her homework – writing fast and furiously.)*

What's she writing? What you writing like that…?

*(**MARGARET** is on the stairs – she starts to sing quietly. She and **JANET** bounce the lines of the Bay City Rollers' "I Only Want to Be with You" between them.)*

*(**PEGGY** puts the plates with fish fingers on the table. **REY** stands completely ignored.)*

PEGGY. Come along, children it's din-dins-time!

> (**REY** *decides. He goes into the hall, disappears for a second and then exclaims.*)

REY. You little monkey!

> (*The TV comes to life. Full volume – the news now. Something about the Yorkshire Ripper.*)

(*Returning.*) Margaret did you play with that chuffing fuse? Listen to your Uncle Rey, I know a thing or two, an' that's an effing dangerous thing for you to be playing with young lady...

PEGGY. (*Ignoring him.*) I think it's time, children, that you sat down to eat. Coming along now!

> (**REY** *switches the TV off.*)

REY. Enough of that. That's not for dinner time, that's not.

> (*Absolutely ignoring* **REY**, **MARGARET** *and* **JIMMY** *troop to the table.* **REY** *looks at them –* **PEGGY** *puts two plates on the table.*)

MARGARET. Jimmy, would you be so kind as to get the ketchup?

JIMMY. You.

> (**REY** *goes upstage into the kitchen, where* **PEGGY** *is fetching the last plate.*)

REY. Let me...

PEGGY. Please, Rey. I just want to be with my children. Please.

> (**MARGARET** *takes her plate to the chair in front of the TV, sits. Eats quickly.*)

Margaret please...

REY. You took that fuse out Margaret! She knows she did.

(A voice at the front door...)

MAURICE. *(Offstage.)* Hello – knockty-knock – anyone at home...?

JIMMY. *(Happy.)* It's M-M-Mr Grosse!

(And he runs to the front door.)

PEGGY. We really should finish our din-dins...

MAURICE. *(Coming in.)* There's my favourite Lieutenant!

> *(He is holding three '99' ice creams [vanilla whippy with chocolate flakes]. **MAURICE** has a smile that lights the place up. He is a kind, gentle man in his mid-sixties, with a bow tie, and good suit. We won't think about it now – but he wears man-made shoes, not leather. The mood lifts. **PEGGY** is all smiles and quickly takes off her apron. The one person who doesn't respond is **JANET**, who hunches over her schoolwork – obsessively writing.)*

PEGGY. Mr Grosse?! We thought you and Mr Playfair were taking the night off?

JIMMY. Mr G-Grosse, I – I – want to s-how you something.

MARGARET. He couldn't keep away – could you, Mr Grosse?!

MAURICE. *(About the ice creams.)* I was passing, matter of fact, Margaret! I hope I'm not interrupting, but I will end up in the dog house if someone doesn't eat these 99s soon! Before they end up on Mrs Hodgson's carpet!

PEGGY. But my ruffians are just about to have their dinner!

MAURICE. Fish fingers *after* ice cream, Mrs Hodgson is quite proper in some circles...

MARGARET. Proper? Like friggen' posh!

MAURICE. *(Laughing.)* I suppose that's right, young Margaret. Yes!

JIMMY. F-f-ish finger and ice c-ream t-ea.

MARGARET. *(To **JIMMY**.)* Why don't you shut your trap.

(She laughs, does 'posh'.) Thank you so very much, Mr Grosse...

> *(She takes an ice cream and wanders to the stairs eating.)*

REY. But Mrs Hodgson's been slaving makin' the nippers their tuck.

PEGGY. Can't do any harm, I suppose.

MAURICE. *(To **JIMMY**.)* Here you go, number two.

> **(JIMMY** *takes his ice cream, eats savouring each lick.)*

JIMMY. W-e h-had all sorts t-oday already, Mr Grosse. The TV went pop.

REY. *(Indulgently.)* Well, someone – someone in this room – fiddled with the fuse, didn't they? Which is not a thing children...

MAURICE. *(Interrupting.)* That's alright – I'm sure I've got some fuses in the back of my car. I appear to have everything including the kitchen sink!

> **(REY** *is stunned –* **MAURICE** *seems not to have heard him...)*

JIMMY. *(Delighted.)* Y-ou d-don't have the k-itchen sink in the car do you, Mr Grosse?!

REY. *(Almost desperate.)* There's nothing wrong with the fuse! Someone just flipped the downstairs ring...

> *(But everyone is ignoring him.* **MAURICE** *holds an ice cream in front of* **JANET**. *He is focused and gentle.)*

MAURICE. This is yours Janet.

PEGGY. What do you say? Girl?

> (**MARGARET** *is watching from behind the sofa.*)

JANET. (*A little voice.*) Thank you Mr Grosse, that's really proper kind.

> (**MAURICE** *smiles. She takes the ice cream and just holds it. Almost as though she has no idea what to do with it. A pause.*)

PEGGY. She's been doin' her studies, haven't you Jan'?

MAURICE. Oh that's a good girl. May I have a look at what you are learni...?

> (*He reaches for* **JANET***'s school book but she puts her hand over it. No negotiation. She then looks him in the eye, for the first time.*)

JANET. Nobody likes a nosey-parker.

> (**MARGARET** *laughs. Loud, out of context.* **MAURICE** *straightens.* **JANET** *takes a single lick of the ice cream.*)

MAURICE. Righto, number two, let's see if we can get that old goggle box working shall we?

REY. It *is* working...

> (*But* **MAURICE** *goes, and* **JIMMY** *follows with his ice cream.* **MARGARET** *has long finished hers.* **JANET** *has abandoned hers; it melts on a plate.* **REY** *decides. He goes across to the table, looks under it and then puts both hands on it. He starts to shake it.* **PEGGY** *now rescues the teapot.*)

PEGGY. Rey, please, you'll break something...

MARGARET. *(Pointing at the armchair, laughing.)* Give us a push, Uncle Rey, and that thing will fly us across the street and into your bedroom. What about that Rey? Into your bed...

REY. *(Almost desperate.)* Peggy, you got to listen to me. He – they – know this is...

> *(**MARGARET** throws herself into the armchair and is singing/shouting at the same time...)*

MARGARET. ...inta' your bed, Rey, hot inta' your arms. I only wanna be with you!

PEGGY. Margaret!

> *(**MARGARET** smiles, and gets out of the chair.)*

REY. Janet you know how you did this, don't you?

> *(He is still shaking the table as **MAURICE** and **JIMMY** come back in. **JIMMY** carries a toolbox, **MAURICE** carries three silver boxes and three camera tripods. **JIMMY** is full of energy.)*

MAURICE. Right, number two – put the tools there, and we can get these upstairs.

> *(**JIMMY** puts the toolbox down by the TV; **PEGGY** smiles – but is uneasy.)*

PEGGY. Mr Grosse?

MAURICE. *(Going upstairs, smiling.)* All shall be revealed! All shall be revealed.

> *(**MAURICE** and **JIMMY** have gone. Upstairs we see movement. **MAURICE** is setting something up, **JIMMY** is enthralled.)*
>
> *(Downstairs –)*

REY. *(Careful.)* Peggy, they been coming here for weeks now. I thought they was taking the night off...

PEGGY. I'll send Margaret round if there's any problems.

MARGARET. That'll be a treat won't it Uncle Rey?

REY. *(Ignoring* **MARGARET**, *whispering.)* He isn't even meant to be here tonight!

PEGGY. Janet, put your homework away, darlin', your dinner's going to be cold.

> *(***JANET** *suddenly turns to* **REY**.*)*

JANET. *(Hard – intense.)* You think this is a zoo, or something? You think we are animals for you to stare at?

> *(***MARGARET** *laughs.)*

REY. I live next door Janet. I'm your neighbour! I lived here all my life.

JANET. Enfield Zoo? An' we are the baba-whatsits??

MARGARET. With them red arses all disgutin' and hangin' out.

> *(***MARGARET** *is on the chair by the TV,* **JANET** *on her chair.)*

JANET. Them baboons!

> *(Both girls scream in excitement and disgust.* **JANET** *laughs, and* **MARGARET** *makes an obscene gesture.)*

PEGGY. Girls, you need to wash your mouths out, talking like that!

REY. Peggy, please...

PEGGY. *(Gently.)* Go home, Rey, have your dinner. Put your feet up. Please.

REY. I care, Peggy.

PEGGY. I know you do.

MARGARET. Sleep tight Uncle Rey.

*(The cat miaows loudly again. A flicker of a
shadow beyond the kitchen window.* **REY** *has
more to say but can't say it. He decides –)*

REY. I'll leave the kitchen door open for Spider.

(Still not wanting to go.) You know where I am…if
anyone needs me.

(He goes. **JIMMY** *thunders down the stairs,
buzzing with excitement.)*

JIMMY. Y-y-ou should see what Mr Grosse has got!

PEGGY. *(Firm.)* It's time, I think, young man, you settled
down and 'ad your evening meal.

(To **MARGARET.**) Girl.

*(***JIMMY** *sits,* **MARGARET** *saunters over.*
JIMMY *wolfs his fish fingers – gone in a
second.* **MARGARET** *then springs up – full of
energy. This is not normal energy.)*

MARGARET. Pardonnez moi –

PEGGY. Margaret. Will you sit down. Now, girl. Please.

*(***MARGARET** *sits – by the TV.* **JIMMY** *eats his
fish fingers.* **MARGARET** *picks whatever is
left on her plate.* **JANET** *just stares at hers.
It's suddenly very quiet, just traffic in the
distance, maybe an ambulance.)*

There. That's better. Who'd like some tea?

(No one says anything.)

Well, I'm going to have myself a nice cuppa.

*(She pours it. Pours in milk, stirs in sugar
[three teaspoons]. Sips.)*

There. Nice.

(*JANET pushes her plate away.*)

Not hungry?

(*JANET opens her exercise book.*)

Jan' please, you worry me, you do.

(*But **JANET** starts to write again, fiercely protecting it from prying eyes. After a moment...*)

MARGARET. (*Whispering.*) Mum, is he coming tonight?

PEGGY. You have your tea. Maybe. I don't know.

(*No one says anything, **JIMMY** and **MARGARET** eat.*)

JIMMY. I-I-I'll tell 'im mum, if h-e-e does. I will.

(***PEGGY** sips her tea. **MAURICE** reappears, down the stairs, that warm smile again...*)

MAURICE. There you all are!

PEGGY. Can I give you a nice cup of tea, Mr Grosse?

MAURICE. Oh Mr Playfair and I have been living in this house – your home – for three, nearly four months, Mrs Hodgson. I do think you can call me Maurice.

PEGGY. I can, but I won't, Mr Grosse, if that's alright with you.

(***MAURICE** smiles, and nods; fair enough.*)

MAURICE. I'm afraid you've only got me tonight. Mr Playfair has some Brazilian psychics visiting. He was picking them up at Heathrow.

(*He glances at his watch and smiles – delighted by the coincidence that he thought of it exactly as Guy was picking up the Brazilians.*)

MAURICE. As we speak! As we speak! This – what has been going on here – has travelled far and wide. I'm sure the Brazilians'll have a thing or two to say about the going ons here...

PEGGY. *(Alarmed.)* Oh, I'm not sure my nerves will hold up. Not with Brazilians on top of everything...

MAURICE. Oh no, they are attending a conference! At The Centre. Guy is excited – this is all marvellous stuff for them. Us mere mortals can only watch with awe. Now, let me see if we can get that goggle box up and running shall we?

> *(As he goes over to the TV, **MARGARET** moves again. This time to the sofa. **MAURICE** switches on the TV and it works [of course]. The TV is showing early evening news – Sex Pistols and, again, the hunt for the Yorkshire Ripper.)*

Well there we are – all ship shape.

JIMMY. It blew up Mr Grosse, like a l-and mine under a Panzer. K-kaboom, Mr Grosse. Achtung, ahhhh.

> *(He throws his arms in the air and then flings himself onto the floor – a dead soldier. **PEGGY** goes into the kitchen.)*

MARGARET. No it friggen' didn't!

JIMMY. *(Shouting.)* She wasn't here. She was on the pardonnez moi...

> *(**PEGGY** is returning with bowls.)*

MAURICE. Two conflicting versions of events! That's quite typical Mr Playfair tells me!

MARGARET. *(Taunting, imitating **JIMMY**.)* It b-blew up l-ike a P-anzer, Mr Grosse! Ach-fart.

JIMMY. M-mum.

PEGGY. Eat your peaches, Jimmy, dear.

(She puts a bowl in front of **JIMMY**. *Tinned peaches and custard.)*

So you grow big and strong like a man.

*(***JIMMY*** eats.)*

An' the custard.

*(***MARGARET*** grabs her peaches but stands eating leaning against the wall...)*

Margaret please...

MAURICE. Now. Upstairs, there are three cameras...

(There are three cameras on tripods in the bedroom.)

With movement sensors. Ever so cunning. You go for one of your little manoeuvres tonight Janet, dear, and Mr Playfair will get a photograph! Or even photographs. Once I've run them through a dark room.

PEGGY. Oh I am not sure...

MAURICE. This equipment is the latest technology, Mrs Hodgson, all the way from Japan. The photographer. You remember Gary that chap from the *Daily Mirror*? Margaret, you remember, Gary?

*(***MARGARET*** blushes.)*

Of course she remembers Gary!

JIMMY. S-she t-ook a shine to Ga...

*(***MARGARET*** whacks **JIMMY** across the head.)*

MARGARET. I'll break your fucking teeth.

PEGGY. Jimmy, you be careful what you say!

*(**MAURICE** sees all this but holds his smile.)*

MAURICE. Well, it was Gary who suggested we should give them a go.

PEGGY. Upstairs?

MAURICE. Mrs Hodgson?

PEGGY. I might need to get up in the night, you know. Never sure when you need...

MAURICE. *(Calming.)* You stay low, Mrs Hodgson, and you'll be AOK.

PEGGY. What do you mean 'stay low'...

MAURICE. Like a commando?

JIMMY. Under t-the b-arbed wire.

*(**JIMMY** starts crawling across the floor. **MAURICE** watches, smiles. Finally...)*

MAURICE. Well. I suppose I better get my skates on. Everything is set up. Jimmy, son, don't you touch anything.

JIMMY. N-n-n-o I won't.

MAURICE. You are my second in command.

*(But **MAURICE** is lingering.)*

PEGGY. You going out? Somewhere, with Mrs Grosse?

MAURICE. *(Surprised.)* Oh I don't expect so. No.

PEGGY. You should. The pictures or something.

*(Everyone but **JANET** is looking at **MAURICE**. She's hunched over her school book.)*

You been here so many nights, Mrs Grosse must be missing you? What will you do, then...?

MAURICE. Oh I think we will...

(Genuinely surprised by the thought.) You know, I don't really know. Isn't that something?

PEGGY. Well there's some tea in the pot. Perhaps I should make it fresh?

MAURICE. Before I go. That would be lovely.

(Lights – but we immediately hear...)

Scene Three

MAURICE ON TAPE. *(Carefully articulating.)* Is there something you want to tell us Janet?

JANET ON TAPE. Grrrrgreeegreewe...

> (**JANET ON TAPE** *sounds very weird – her voice is mixed with a man's voice. A growl, almost a bark. Listen to the tapes...*)

> *(It is dark outside. Just the yellow haze of a street lamp – lights from a couple of houses further down the street.* **MAURICE** *has the table in the centre of the room – under the central light. He has his jacket off but wears his braces and his bow tie. A reel-to-reel tape recorder is on the table in front of him. He has huge headphones on. A pad of paper is near him. An old cup of tea, the teapot.)*

MAURICE ON TAPE. I am going to ask you again. What is your name?

JANET ON TAPE. MRGGGRWILGGGGGKENSTOYOU SHITDARK.

> *(Sounds of* **JIMMY** *giggling on the tape.)*

JIMMY ON TAPE. Sounds like she's doing a poo!

MARGARET ON TAPE. Will you shut your cake hole!

MAURICE ON TAPE. No need for language, please children...

> (**JANET** *screams on the tape.*)

What the blazes!

> (**MAURICE** *stops the tape, winds it back. Plays again.)*

MARGARET ON TAPE. ...you shut your cake hole.

MAURICE ON TAPE. No need for language, please children...

> (**JANET***'s scream again.* **MAURICE** *stops the tape.*)

MAURICE. *(Reading back what he has written.)* "Immediately after Margaret Hodgson spoke something hit Janet very hard. Sometime later, after the young woman had calmed down, I found a Lego brick – that's a plastic building toy for the uninitiated – on the carpet..."

(He holds a little Lego brick.) "...In and of itself, the toy weighs barely an ounce..."

(Slight pause , he then starts to write again.) "...someone or something...threw the brick with a velocity... It caused Janet Hodgson to scream, and left a very nasty mark."

> *(He stops – this matters to him.)*

"On her head. I then continued with my interviews..."

> *(He puts the headphones back on. And plays the tape.)*

MAURICE ON TAPE. Does it hurt, Janet – where the brick hit you...?

> (**MAURICE** *continues downstairs, oblivious as the flash bulbs go upstairs.*)

JANET ON TAPE. Grggggrgeooooogret...

> *(Upstairs –)*

> *(Flash –* **JANET** *is in the air. With every move, the cameras flash.)*

> *(Flash –* **JANET** *is two feet above the bed.)*

(It's like a strobe effect. It is a nightmare.)

(Downstairs –)

*(**MAURICE** hears nothing because of the headphones.)*

MAURICE ON TAPE. *(Calm.)* Janet, I'd like you to answer me. Are you in pain? Please, it would be most helpful to understand...

JANET ON TAPE. (Interrupting.) Grrrreherehgeggggg...

(Maurice's tape continues downstairs as:)

(Upstairs –)

*(Flash – **PEGGY** wakes.)*

*(She has been sleeping with the children, with **JANET** beside her in a double bed, **JIMMY** on a camp-bed, **MARGARET** on a truckle bed. **PEGGY** is in a very modest nightie, **JANET** is in pink, and **MARGARET** is in something a little skimpy.)*

(Downstairs –)

*(The tape continues downstairs. **MAURICE** hears nothing because of the headphones.)*

JANET ON TAPE. Gerrtoutofhere...

MAURICE ON TAPE. Janet – can you tell me where you are, please?

JANET ON TAPE. Grratoutofereyougrrrrrr. Greee...

MARGARET ON TAPE. *(Laughing.)* Grrrfartgrafart...

MAURICE ON TAPE. *(As **JANET**'s voice continues.)* Please, Margaret! Janet, are you at home? Are you somewhere safe?

JANET ON TAPE. Grrrrrleavemefuckingrrrrralone.

MAURICE ON TAPE. Janet? Can tell me who you are? Do you have a name?

MARGARET ON TAPE. *(Laughing.)* Ghosts don't 'ave names, do they!

MAURICE ON TAPE. Please, Margaret!

JANET ON TAPE. G-G-G...

MAURICE ON TAPE. G? Is that a G?

JANET ON TAPE. H. G-H...

MAURICE ON TAPE. G-H?

MARGARET ON TAPE. O! Betcha...

MAURICE ON TAPE. *(Gently.)* Jan'?

JANET ON TAPE. O-S-

MARGARET ON TAPE. T. *(Laughing, but uneasy.)* She is spelling GHOS...

> *(Maurice's tape continues while...)*
>
> *(Upstairs –)*
>
> *(Flash –* **PEGGY** *realises, to her horror, that* **JANET** *is not beside her.)*
>
> *(Flash –* **MARGARET** *is now waking.)*
>
> *(Flash –* **JANET** *appears to be being pulled out the door.* **PEGGY** *is sitting on the double bed. She sees* **JANET**. **MARGARET** *turns to see* **JANET**.)*
>
> *(Downstairs –* **MAURICE** *looks up. The ceiling light is swinging. Mystified, he pulls off the headphones.)*
>
> *(Upstairs – Flash –* **PEGGY** *is screaming.* **JIMMY** *wakes.* **JANET** *is being pulled out of the window at the top of the stairs with the curtain around her neck. It's horrific.)*

(**MARGARET** *is frozen with fear against a wall in the bedroom.*)

(**JIMMY**, *in flannel pyjamas, runs to the top of the stairs and comes down – shouting...*)

JIMMY. M-M-r-Grosse it's t-trying to k-ill J-anet!

(**MAURICE** *leaps up. As he moves, the teapot falls off the table and shatters. He sees the broken pot but runs to the bottom of the stairs...*)

PEGGY. *(Screaming.)* It's trying to kill her Mr Grosse!

MAURICE. It's alright, it's alright. I am here.

PEGGY. It's tryin' to drag her out the window!

(**MAURICE** *runs up the stairs and takes* **JANET***'s weight.*)

MAURICE. Give me a hand, take her weight!

(**MAURICE** *calls.*) You too Margaret, if you don't mind.

(**MARGARET** *runs to* **MAURICE** *and* **PEGGY.** **JANET**, *who is writhing, apparently being strangled.* **MAURICE**, **PEGGY** *and* **MARGARET** *take her weight.*)

JIMMY. *(Barely able to speak.)* Mr Grosse...

PEGGY. Help her, please.

MAURICE. I've got her. We got her! Margaret, the curtain – right away – that's a good girl.

(**MARGARET** *struggles to pull the curtain away from* **JANET***'s throat.* **JANET** *gasps for breath.*)

Let's get her downstairs. There we are. It's all alright, Mrs Hodgson.

(**JIMMY** *backs down the stairs as* **MARGARET** *and* **MAURICE** *carry* **JANET** *down,* **PEGGY** *follows.*)

PEGGY. Whatever is the time?

MAURICE. It's not even eleven!

MARGARET. He's early tonight!

MAURICE. Careful. There we are. You are alright, Janet.

PEGGY. Every night. Every night.

(*At the bottom of the stairs,* **MAURICE** *and* **MARGARET** *take* **JANET** *to the sofa.* **PEGGY** *leans in – her hand on* **JANET**'s *head.* **JIMMY** *watches ashen from the bottom of the stairs.*)

Feel her head: she's hot – she's on fire! The fire – Mr Grosse...!

JIMMY. (*Terrified.*) Is Jan' going to die, Mr Grosse?

MAURICE. Oh no. No one's going to die, number two. Not on my watch!

(**PEGGY** *runs to the kitchen – fast and purposeful.* **JANET** *moans.*)

PEGGY. Let me fetch something to cool her down.

(**JANET** *stirs –* **MAURICE** *is clearly relieved. All the strength he has shown now looks like a front.*)

MAURICE. So, looks as though we are in the land of the living Janet...

JANET. I feel sick.

MARGARET. (*Relieved.*) Jan' you OK? Fuckin' 'ell that scared the shit out of me, that did.

(**PEGGY** *is returning with a soaked hand towel.*)

PEGGY. Mr Grosse is here, Margaret, please wash your mouth out. She doesn't mean that Mr Grosse...

(She sees the broken teapot.)

Oh my, whatever happened...

MAURICE. Our poltergeist is no respecter of crockery, sadly, Mrs Hodgson. I'll nip out for a new one the moment the shops on the parade open in the morning.

> *(**JIMMY** now sits on the stairs. **MARGARET** crosses to him.)*

MARGARET. It's alright Jimmy boy. He's white as a sheet, mum. Look at him!

> *(**MARGARET** sits beside **JIMMY**. After a moment, he is asleep – his head on her lap. **MARGARET** strokes his hair tenderly.)*

PEGGY. I am glad you stayed, after all, I am.

*(She carefully wraps the hand towel around **JANET**'s head.)*

MAURICE. I am too. I really am. What a thing. That looked really quite serious...

PEGGY. I thought 'it' was going to take her.

There we go...

> *(She's finished tying the hand towel around **JANET**'s head.)*

MAURICE. The poor chil...

> *(He stops himself. **MAURICE** has pulled back from **JANET** and stares at her. **PEGGY** turns back to him.)*

PEGGY. Mr Grosse are you alright?

(He snaps out of the stare, and smiles, but is rattled.)

MAURICE. Oh golly, yes I'm sorry! Night after night is beginning to take its toll.

PEGGY. *(Gently.)* Why don't you go home? The traffic will have stopped by now. I can look after the nippers. I can.

*(He looks again at **JANET**, turns and smiles at **PEGGY**.)*

MAURICE. I wonder if we should keep to ourselves that I am here without Guy? You know, really this is HIS case. Mr Playfair is the expert, and I am just the enthusiastic amateur. He's seen all sorts, all over the world. I'd hate him to think that I somehow was going behind his back, or something equally bonkers.

(Change.) It is really quite remarkable some of the tales he has to tell... what he has seen! Listen to me chattering away. I'd better sweep up that teapot.

*(**MAURICE** stands.)*

PEGGY. No, you stay with Jan'.

MAURICE. No, please, I am the guilty party when it comes to your teap...

*(He peters out. They are both uneasy. Finally, **PEGGY** whispers –)*

PEGGY. *(Very serious.)* It scares me, Mr Grosse. To be near her. After. Please.

*(**JIMMY** stirs – loud...)*

JIMMY. D-d-don't do that, don't do that...

MARGARET. He's only having a friggin' nightmare, mum, silly sausage.

PEGGY. Well, let's get you all to bed.

MAURICE. Yes. Yes. Everyone needs some sleep. I'll keep an eye on Jan'. I'll pop upstairs with her when she's feeling more herself.

> (**PEGGY** *moves to the stairs. She touches* **JIMMY**'s *sleeping face.*)

PEGGY. He's as pale as a ghost.

MARGARET. *(Quietly.)* Is Mr Grosse staying?

PEGGY. Come on young lady.

> (*She shepherds* **MARGARET** *and* **JIMMY** *[half-asleep] up to the bedroom.* **MAURICE** *is downstairs. Finally, he glances over his shoulder: no one is on the stairs. He hesitates. His breathing is intense. He goes to* **JANET** *on the sofa and kneels in front of her.*)

MAURICE. *(Very quietly.)* Janet, Janet...?

> (*What he doesn't realise is that* **MARGARET** *has come back down the stairs and is crossing the room on tiptoes, when suddenly she cries...*)

MARGARET. Owwww. Something just cut me fuckin' toe off!

> (**MAURICE** *turns, alarmed.*)

MAURICE. Margaret? What on earth are you doing?

MARGARET. I am bleedin' half to death.

MAURICE. *(Standing, rattled.)* What were you doing? Creeping around like that?

MARGARET. This is bad, a bad cut. Blood an' stuff.

MAURICE. Oh dear let me have a look – we seem to have lost the teapot to our friend and I was going to sweep...

(He moves towards her – she grins at him.)

MARGARET. What were you doing? Just then, with Jan'?

MAURICE. Oh. I was worried I heard Janet sort of... *(He makes a ggrrrrrr noise.)* Always frightened she might bite her tongue off or something equally horrible.

MARGARET. Well that would shut her gob at least!

(Her foot.) This hurts like very, very, very badly, Mr Grosse. Seriously bad.

MAURICE. Let me get it cleaned up. And I'd better sweep up this old...

> *(He goes up to the kitchen. **MARGARET** stands, hops across to **JANET**. Leans over – prods her. She whispers a line from the Bay City Rollers' "I Only Want to Be with You". But **JANET** doesn't react. **MARGARET** frowns. Something is not right. **MAURICE** appears carrying a tea towel, dustpan and brush.)*

Let the poor child rest; this is all taking it out of her, I'd say.

MARGARET. *(Turning.)* What is 'this', Mr Grosse?

MAURICE. Sit here, young lady.

> *(**MARGARET** hops up to a chair **MAURICE** has pulled out. She sits. **MAURICE** kneels, looks at the cut on **MARGARET**'s foot.)*

Not fatal, but going to be sore...

MARGARET. You are ticklin' me!

MAURICE. Well we have got to get this cleaned up. Now Margaret (off to bed)...

MARGARET. *(Interrupting.)* D'you really think this house is haunted?

MAURICE. *(Laughing.)* If it's not, I'm not honestly sure what I and Mr Playfair are doing here night after night!

MARGARET. Oh some of them think we are chancing it – don't they? That lady, an' the bloke, they thought we were chancing it, didn't they?

MAURICE. *(Laughing.)* After all the attention this house is getting the Society for Psychical Research are duty bound to be sceptical. There are a terrifying amount of lunatics out there claiming they are haunted. Granted, most don't get the front page of the *Daily Mirror* or on the British Bellyache Corporation but usually things like this...

MARGARET. *(Interrupting.)* They seen things like this before, they said? And?

MAURICE. And?

MARGARET. And what do they reckon is going to happen, clever clogs?

> (**MARGARET** *looks at him – intent. She then smiles.*)

We – was Jan's idea – we were messin' when the toilet door got locked on the inside.

MAURICE. Yes, we knew, gave us quite a chuckle.

> (**MARGARET** *didn't expect that.*)

And you hid my tape recorder and said the poltergeist had it.

MARGARET. We never!

MAURICE. So why were you and Janet whispering and laughing on the tape? The record button is the red one.

> (**MAURICE** *has moved away.*)

MARGARET. Them papers reckon it's real, don't they? They certainly think it's real.

MAURICE. One might argue that they rather like to say it's real. You know to sell. But, yes, indeed. There has been an awful lot of interest in what we've all been up to here at number 284 Green Street! Now bed, young lady.

(**MARGARET** *stands, balancing her sore foot by holding onto a chair.*)

MARGARET. Do you like what you see?

MAURICE. Oh that cut should be fine, Margaret. Now I think it's bed...

MARGARET. No I meant me...

(*She twists – a sort of uncertain sexiness.*)

The woman in front of you, Mr Grosse.

MAURICE. (*Embarrassed.*) Oh. Naturally. Yes. Of course. You are charming Margaret.

MARGARET. Or Jimmy, do you like Jimmy?

MAURICE. Jimmy?

MARGARET. Well – you know – like a shirt lifter, being posh an'all.

MAURICE. No really no.

MARGARET. Oh cummon, Mr Grosse you are here all the time – night and day – what do you want from us? We got nothing.

MAURICE. It's the case. Besides, Guy and I want to help.

(**PEGGY** *is on the stairs – she looks exhausted but is listening.*)

I... we are trying to support you and your mother and Janet and Jimmy, through something that is extremely tiresome.

MARGARET. Bollocks.

MAURICE. *(Shocked.)* We *are* trying to help. Now...

MARGARET. Are you? Really? Or do you just *like* bein' here? You know everything about us. Mebbe you got nowhere else to go?

> (**MAURICE** *stares at her – he's stung. Then she laughs.)*

I don't mean nothin' serious, Mr Grosse. Fuckin' 'ell look at you!

MAURICE. Please, my dear.

MARGARET. Pardonnez moi.

MAURICE. Yes, that's a jolly good idea.

> *(But she moves towards* **MAURICE**.*)*

MARGARET. *(About her nightie.)* Dad says if this was any shorter, it would put men in prison. What d'you reckon?

> *(And she turns and sees* **PEGGY** *sat at the bottom of the stairs.)*

PEGGY. *(Firm, angry.)* Get yourself to the toilet and then bed Margaret. Bed.

> (**MARGARET** *moves fast to the toilet.* **PEGGY** *doesn't even look at* **MAURICE** *as she picks up the dustpan and brush and starts sweeping up the broken teapot.)*

MAURICE. Oh, I can do that...

> *(But* **PEGGY** *doesn't stop. There is a flush, and* **MARGARET** *emerges from the loo and hurries upstairs. After a moment,* **MAURICE** *crosses to* **JANET** *and puts his hand on her wrist.)*

That's better. She's cooler – at first it was – is like she's on fire...

(**PEGGY** *makes herself busy clearing up the broken china.*)

PEGGY. The child's right you know. You know all about us – too much some might say, you and Mr Playfair and I don't know nothin' about you. You got the car – the Jaguar, an' you certainly don't count your pennies, don't get me wrong – but we don't know nothing about you.

MAURICE. Oh I'm not sure what there is to know.

PEGGY. No. Mr Grosse. Margaret's a girl. Just a girl. You should've sent her to bed straight away. Straightaway.

MAURICE. I was... I meant...

(**PEGGY** *has made her point and gets back to sweeping up.*)

(*Trying again.*) You have been very kind, Mrs Hodgson, really, and I'm s...

PEGGY. (*Sharp.*) Oh I thought it was you being kind? I thought *you* was helping us?

MAURICE. It's a form of words...

PEGGY. But Mr Playfair is the expert?

MAURICE. Oh yes. He's your man on ghosts and poltergeists, as you have seen.

PEGGY. Suppose he is.

MAURICE. And I'm just a hanger-on.

PEGGY. So what's all this?

(*She points at the tape recorder and notes on the kitchen table.*)

MAURICE. My role – if that isn't too grand – is to record. Notate. For the big cheeses.

(**PEGGY** *wants more.*)

MAURICE. I am technical, you know. After my time in the services my career has been technical. Scientific. A bit of an inventor if truth be told. I think things either are or they are not. You make something with wings and a bloody great engine or two and you have an airliner, or you don't.

PEGGY. So, we are some kind of scientific whats it called?

MAURICE. Oh golly no! No. Mr Playfair is genuinely concerned. And my job is to make sure everything is recorded. This happened then. At this time. That event then…

PEGGY. And them cameras?! I'm going to have words when he comes tomorrow. In the nippers' bedroom!

MAURICE. Yes, maybe we should…

PEGGY. Should?

MAURICE. Maybe that is too far.

PEGGY. And he's talking to a conference you say?

MAURICE. Experts.

PEGGY. Experts from Brazil?

MAURICE. And others. There's a great deal of interest. I think they are doing a lecture…

PEGGY. *(Deeply alarmed.)* I don't like the idea of experts from Brazil doing a lecture. A lecture about us? I don't think we should be talked about, I don't. What can they know, that I don't know?

*(Slight pause. **PEGGY** now has a full dust-pan.)*

Nothing.

*(She takes the dustpan into the kitchen, empties it into the bin. After her questioning **MAURICE** is uneasy. He goes to his notes and equipment. He tidies things up. He then smiles – a change of tack.)*

MAURICE. You know, I wonder why we don't talk to the Council. See if we can get you away from here? To another house? Or perhaps a flat? They can be lovely...

PEGGY. *(Interrupting, firm.)* No, Mr Grosse, I'm not having that.

MAURICE. *(Rising to his theme.)* But everything stopped when we got you down to the seaside! The sea air did you all the world of good. And I have to say you were very different people on your return...

PEGGY. I will not give in to him. I will not.

MAURICE. Peggy, marriages fail. It is sad, terribly sad...

PEGGY. It didn't 'fail'. Eddie tore my heart out and spat it back in my face.

MAURICE. So move! He only comes here to collect his social. He's lying and I've seen what he does...

PEGGY. *(Sharp.)* The child's here, Mr Grosse.

> (**JANET** *is fast asleep.* **PEGGY** *whispers...*)

They love their father. Proper. They do.

> *(Beat.)*

I will not give in. I know what you think, but if I give in to him, if I run from my home I won't have anything left. Not even my dignity.

MAURICE. He's a monster. I'm sorry to use that language but he is and he terrifies the children.

> (**PEGGY** *turns away from* **MAURICE**, *angry. A loud miaow from the kitchen and a shadow of a black cat looms large.* **PEGGY** *scurries into the kitchen. She opens the back window –)*

PEGGY. *(Upstage, to the cat.)* Will you go away, Spider there's nothing for you here.

*(**MAURICE** turns – **JANET** has sat bolt upright. She has the towel wrapped around her head.)*

JANET. Daddy.

MAURICE. Janet?

*(**PEGGY** returning.)*

PEGGY. That cat will drive us all into an asylum long before your poltergeist does.

*(**MAURICE** turns to her.)*

Rey doesn't feed that poor mite. She's miaowing night and day.

*(**MAURICE** turns back – **JANET** is fast asleep again.)*

(Alarmed.) Mr Grosse?

(He sits.)

Mr Grosse?

(He is unable to speak.)

Let me get you some water.

MAURICE. Yes, yes please.

*(She goes. He looks back at **JANET** who seems fast asleep. He is mystified.)*

(Trying to rally.) Oh golly.

PEGGY. Here we go.

*(She gives **MAURICE** the water. He's very rattled. He takes a drink and then another gulp. Finally...)*

MAURICE. I was only passing this evening, you know, when I saw the ice cream van.

PEGGY. *(Indulgent.)* You, in Enfield, *passing*, Mr Grosse?

(**MAURICE** *tries to smile.*)

MAURICE. I wanted to... well...

(Serious.) I'd rather Mr Playfair didn't know I popped by tonight.

(**PEGGY** *smiles – and sits.*)

PEGGY. Think you said that now, Mr Grosse, enough times for even me to get the message. You feeling any better?

MAURICE. Probably a little over-tired.

PEGGY. Nothing like your own bed.

MAURICE. Oh I wouldn't sleep anyway.

(He stands – wanders. He keeps glancing back to **JANET**.*)*

PEGGY. So what do you think is going on, Mr Grosse?

MAURICE. I suggest Mr Playfair...

PEGGY. He doesn't talk to someone like me. Well not in any way a normal person can understand! All them portals, and chance matter...

(Slight pause.)

I do get frightened.

MAURICE. Of him?

PEGGY. No, no.

(She tries to shake away the thought but then finally says it.)

I am frightened of losing Jan', Mr Grosse. Am I...?

MAURICE. *(Interrupting.)* Oh we won't let anything like that happen. That won't happen.

PEGGY. I couldn't bear to lose her.

> *(Slight pause.)*

I'd rather myself die than see anything happen to any of my nippers. You can understand that?

> *(**MAURICE** looks at her, nods. **PEGGY** has Janet's school book.)*

You seen the way she does this?

> *(She opens the school book.)*

(Startled.) What's this?

> *(**MAURICE** takes the book – he looks at the pages.)*

MAURICE. There's just…

PEGGY. She's not writing nothing. Just like she's scratching. Scratching.

> *(Leafing through page after page…)*

MAURICE. I'm sure there's an explanation, Mr Play…

PEGGY. *(Interrupting.)* Is she doin' that at school? You heard what they are sayin' at school about us? Them children, they hate us. Say we trying to *be* something. Margaret's old enough but Jan'… What does it mean? What is happenin' to her? She's not eating, and look at this – she's just… I don't know. I don't know. I want it to stop.

MAURICE. That's what we are all trying to sort…

PEGGY. No, I mean: is it me? Is it me? Is it him? What have the nippers seen? Oh.

(**MAURICE** *mops his brow with his handkerchief. He's out of his depth,* **PEGGY** *is emotional.*)

MAURICE. I'm sure it's not you...

PEGGY. I just want it all to stop. It all to stop. Him storming in here drunk, Brazilians talking about us. I want it to stop. And look at Jan' – look at her. Sorry, Mr Grosse. Sorry, but Mr Playfair told us about the fire – the fire that comes in the end...

MAURICE. Oh only very rarely. Not usually.

PEGGY. And that the little girl in Brazil was burnt up...

MAURICE. (*Interrupting.*) As a worst-case scenario. And that was in Brazil.

PEGGY. (*Loud, raw.*) But is what's happening to her the worst-case? Is this the worst case?!

(*Slight pause.* **MAURICE** *knows he's got to answer* **PEGGY**.)

MAURICE. Well, what, actually, Guy said – if I got this right – was that these things build and build. That the paranormal activity comes to a kind of head, or a crisis – and then they go. No excuse, no pack drill.

(**PEGGY** *stares at him – she wants more.*)

Only in the most rare – most terrible instances, in Brazil, for example, not here, certainly not in Enfield, and only sometimes the... well, the person to whom... combusts.

PEGGY. Jan'?

MAURICE. Definitely not.

(**PEGGY** *puts the school book back on the table near Maurice's tape recorder.*)

MAURICE. *(Gently.)* Get some sleep. Go on, you go up. Janet is quite safe with me. I'll stay awake. You need to keep up with your sleep...

> (**PEGGY** *stands.*)

PEGGY. Thank you. I'm not sure what I would do without you. Both.

MAURICE. And I'm not sure I would know what to do without you.

> *(He wishes he hadn't said that.* **PEGGY** *is looking at him. Uneasy, he smiles his smile.)*

Retired! With too flippin' much time on my own! This, at least, is keeping me out of mischief.

PEGGY. But what about Mrs Grosse? Doesn't she wonder at you being out every night?

MAURICE. Betty? Oh no she's got the garden, and her whist.

PEGGY. Well so long as she doesn't think we've stolen you.

MAURICE. *(Smiling.)* Oh no. Gosh no.

PEGGY. And you have children. A boy, at least. I can tell. The way you play with our Jimmy. He just lights up when you are here and all the talk of Panzers and Stukas...

MAURICE. I rather hope I haven't exaggerated my experiences, but I suppose a little bit of war leaves an indelible mark on a man.

PEGGY. But no girls?

> (**JANET** *stirs.*)

JANET. Mum, sorry mum. I been asleep.

> *(She looks at* **MAURICE**.*)*

Mr Grosse? What the heck are you doin' here?

PEGGY. He is staying downstairs to keep us all safe, aren't you Maurice?

MAURICE. I am, I am. And I had some work to catch up with. In the quiet.

JANET. He's very brave – ain't you Mr Grosse – from the war.

MAURICE. *(Blushing.)* Well. To be honest I thought you were asleep when I was boring your dear mother...

> *(**JANET** puts an arm out. **MAURICE** helps her to stand.)*

PEGGY. Let's get you upstairs my little lady.

> *(**PEGGY** moves to **JANET** and holds her. Over **PEGGY**'s shoulder, **JANET** stares intensely at **MAURICE**.)*

MAURICE. Janet?

> *(And she shuts her eyes tight shut. **PEGGY** holds her as she takes her to the stairs. The cat miaows outside.)*

PEGGY. Bed.

> *(**PEGGY** goes on holding **JANET** as they go up the stairs.)*

Mr Grosse...

> *(He goes to them and helps **PEGGY** and **JANET** up the stairs.)*

Shhh, now we don't want to wake the nippers. It's late.

MAURICE. It is. It is the witching hours.

> *(They are in the bedroom – but bend very low so they don't fire the flash bulbs. **JIMMY** stirs.)*

PEGGY. You go back to sleep Jimmy.

JIMMY. Mr Grosse c-an c-an you tell us about them Stuka dive bombers again.

MAURICE. That will save until the morning...

*(Then, suddenly **MARGARET** sits bolt upright and shouts.)*

MARGARET. No, no. Please, mum, don't let him do that!

(And she triggers the flash bulbs. Flash! Flash! Flash!)

PEGGY. Maggie Maggie, it's alright, darlin'.

*(To **MAURICE**.)* Just a nightmare.

MAURICE. Everyone be still.

*(Downstairs – Suddenly, a **MAN** is in the living room. We only see him for a split second.)*

(He is missing a leg and leans heavily on a crutch. A filthy bandage is wrapped around his hand, where it has blistered from the crutch. He is wearing what was once an old hospital gown and pyjama trousers. One pyjama leg is tied up over his stump. Everything about him is filthy. This is more than unwashed. Dirt has made his skin, his clothes, everything black and oily. It is almost as though he has risen from a grave... His mouth is open in an agonising – but silent – scream.)

(And almost as soon as we have seen him, a very loud bang kicks us in the guts and is instantly followed by a total blackout.)

PEGGY. *(Whispering – terrified.)* What's happened? It's pitch black.

MAURICE. I don't know. It must be another power cut. I can't see any of the other houses, and the street li... Shhhhh.

PEGGY. What?

MAURICE. I can hear movement – or something. Downstairs –

PEGGY. Mr Grosse?

MAURICE. Yes?

PEGGY. Is that you holding my hand?

MAURICE. I jolly well hope so!

> (*They both start to giggle.*)

MARGARET. (*Whispering in the dark.*) What's going on?

MAURICE. (*Laughing.*) Our friend now appears to have knocked all the power out in North London!

> (*A match is struck. Then a candle lit.*)

PEGGY. I keep it here in case I need the pardonnez moi in the night, Mr Grosse and don't want to put the light on.

MAURICE. Good thinking, Mrs Hodgson.

> (**PEGGY** *holds the candle up. Just enough light to see.*)

MAURICE. I think I've got an old torch in my toolbox downstairs. You alright, Mrs Hodgson, if I go downstairs?

PEGGY. I don't much like the dark.

MAURICE. (*He doesn't either.*) No. Well. Wish me luck.

> (*He sets off down the stairs. Just a hint of light now as his eyes adjust. Downstairs, something large is in the middle of the living room.*)

MAURICE. *(To himself.)* Hello? Anyone there?

> *(He bumps into the armchair, which is not where he thought it was and panics himself...)*

Oh crumbs.

> *(He stumbles and then finds his tool kit.)*

Ah there we are – there we are.

> *(He switches on the torch. The gas fire is in the middle of the living room floor.* **MAURICE** *swings the torch over to the fireplace – the fire has been violently ripped out of the tiled surround, some bricks have come with it.* **MAURICE** *talks to himself to keep his courage up.)*

What a thing. Will you look at that – it's only ripped the gas fire out of the hearth!

> *(He goes nearer. Bends and tries to lift the iron fire but can't. Then he goes back to the fireplace – looks in... there's a hissing noise.)*

A smell of gas. A gas leak.

(Suddenly realising, horrified.) Fire! The fire – the fire burnt the girl!

> *(***MAURICE** *doesn't know what to do. He turns, panicking but freezes when there's a quiet TAP-TAP-TAP upstage.* **MAURICE** *spins.)*

Who's that? Who's there?

> *(Upstairs –)*

MARGARET. Oh, no. It's dad, mum!

PEGGY. Come here girl.

> *(***MARGARET** *and* **JIMMY** *are wrapped in* **PEGGY***'s arms.* **JANET** *is fast asleep.)*

(Downstairs –)

MAURICE. Who is it?

> *(The TAP-TAP-TAP on the door is louder. Then the letter box flaps open.)*

REY. Peggy, Peg'? Are you OK?

> *(The front door opens. **REY** comes in carefully – ready, he thinks, for anything. He holds a torch – it dazzles **MAURICE**.)*

Well, well, what are you doing here Mr Grosse? It's one thirty in the morning.

> *(He holds up his key.)*

Mrs Hodgson gave me a key. For emergencies and I'd say all the power goin' down in Enfield is an emergency, wouldn't you, Mr Grosse?

> *(His torch swings to the stove.)*

By all the Saints an' friends of the devil – what the heck is the stove doin' there?

MAURICE. *(Urgent.)* Do you know where the gas main is, Rey?

REY. I do.

MAURICE. The stove was ripped from the wall.

REY. Who on earth would do that?

MAURICE. *(Urgent.)* The gas?

> *(**REY** sniffs.)*

REY. You've got a leak or something. That could be extremely serious. A match or a candle and the whole...

MAURICE. Where is it?

REY. What Mr Grosse? We have a gas hazard which is...

MAURICE. *(Loud.)* The mains? The shut off?

> *(**REY** stares at **MAURICE** – finally the penny drops.)*

REY. No need to shout. Keep your hair on. It's under the stairs – next to the meter – for future reference.

> *(As **REY** goes to under the stairs, the lights come on – boom – boom – boom – concluding with the street lights. It is immediately clear the living room is a mess. The stove, the armchair etc.)*

(Calling from inside the cupboard.) Twist and then up. Though I very much hope there won't be a future reference. I reckon, Mr Grosse, these Unions and their strikes are...

PEGGY. Oh Lord – it's really had a go tonight.

> *(**MAURICE** turns to **PEGGY**, who has come down the stairs. **REY** appears from the cupboard.)*

MAURICE. We will get the place tidied up, Peggy, in no time, won't we Rey?

REY. We certainly will. Let's all have a nice cuppa!

PEGGY. We got no teapot.

MAURICE. And you've just turned off the gas.

REY. Me and my big mouth.

> *(He grins, looks at the stove.)*

That is quite a thing, that is.

(Carefully.) You reckon, Mr Grosse, we can get this out of the way? Be awful if there was an accident, with everythin' else that's going on.

PEGGY. Leave it – we can –

MAURICE. No, Rey is right. Someone trips over that and... well, our poltergeist will be one up.

PEGGY. I reckon he's winning anyway, Mr Grosse.

MAURICE. *(Positive.)* Cummon, let's see what you are made of Rey.

(*He goes to the stove.*)

REY. Back alright?

(*They both take either side of the stove.*)

A man like you is not going to welcome a hernia.

MAURICE. On my three.

REY. One two three.

(*And they can't lift it.*)

PEGGY. Leave it there. We can tell the children to be careful.

REY. If you, Mr Grosse, were able to take a bit more of the...

PEGGY. *(Don't.)* Please, Mr Grosse...

MAURICE. I can do it.

PEGGY. You go home with a slipped whatsisname and there'll be hell to pay! We can clean up in the morning, thank you Rey.

(**REY** *turns to* **PEGGY**.)

REY. When the power went out I thought – you were my first thought – I'd better get round and check how Peggy is doing. I like to help people. I want to be a good person...but none of us are saints are we Mr Grosse? Nobody would call me a saint...but I'd like to think that I am a good person.

(*He looks at the gas fire in the middle of the room.*)

PEGGY. Well. I think we should all get some sleep.

REY. *(Interrupting.)* This is a nice street, Mr Grosse.

> (**MAURICE** *turns – startled by the change in*
> **REY***'s tone.)*

PEGGY. Don't start Rey, not now...

REY. *(Interrupting.)* An ordinary street. There's nothing special about Enfield, or this street. And I think we need this to stop.

(Change.) Anyway, I'm at work in the morning. You safe as houses now with the gas off, Peggy. You staying Mr Grosse?

> (**REY** *points at the tape recorder.)*

That is quite a piece of kit, that is Mr Grosse? German?

MAURICE. I'm afraid so. I had work to do Rey.

REY. I thought you were just passing?

> (**MAURICE** *doesn't blanch and turns back to*
> *the tape recorder.)*

MAURICE. It is very accurate and you can switch it to different speeds – hear things, you know, that you might not always hear with the human ear. It's all quite fascinating.

PEGGY. Well, I'm going to turn in...

> *(But* **REY** *still doesn't go.)*

REY. This room – I must say – the whole house, truth be told, is full of memories.

(He grins.) When I was a lad, my best mate lived here. Can't begin to tell you what we got up to. Well, I can but I'd have to kill you after.

> *(He laughs at his own joke.)*

PEGGY. *(Quiet.)* Rey, please, this is not the time...

REY. *(Interrupting.)* Terry Wilkins. What he went through. His father – he sat there smoking. He lost his leg at the hospital when it went, you know, and, you excuse my language, he was pissing, couldn't control his... *(Waterworks.)* Then he went blind. He was cursing an' roaring until one day Terry and his mum just *disappeared*. Gone. We used to say maybe the old bastard buried them in the garden!

> *(He laughs at the thought.)*

You see Mr Grosse, round here, we are neighbours. Ordinary people. Me, Peggy, her nippers. Like Terry, and his mother. You short of something, Peggy, and Rey is here for you, you know that. And I reckon...

> *(The cat miaows in the garden or somewhere,*
> **REY** *laughs.)*

I'll be found with that cat in a bag somewhere near the canal one of these days. But Mr Grosse, so, you tell us: what d'you and Mr Playfair reckon?

> *(**MAURICE** looks to **PEGGY**.)*

Mr Playfair. He's a right odd one, your friend, isn't he? But listen: we don't like having the wool pulled, you see, around here.

PEGGY. *(Snapping.)* Rey, will you please go home.

> *(**REY** blushes.)*

REY. Sorry, Peg' but I'm just asking...

MAURICE. I am not the expert.

PEGGY. Go home, Rey.

> *(**REY** looks at **PEGGY** and then turns back to*
> **MAURICE**. *He's not leaving without an answer.)*

MAURICE. Portals.

>   (**REY** *isn't satisfied.*)

Energy. Windows. Between worlds.

REY. In Enfield?

MAURICE. Between the dead and the living.

REY. Fuck off! Excuse my language, Peggy, but I don't
believe a word of it. Mr Grosse d'you know what people
are saying?

MAURICE. Peggy, I should come back in the morning,
when everyone feels a little more like it.

REY. *Nothing* is happening. Them girls, I'm sorry, and you
and Mr Playfair and the rest, it's like you just get them
excited. And then the TV and the papers and the like
and who can say stop? Who can say this is all a load of
old bollocks?

MAURICE. The gas fire?

REY. The girls did that, I reckon. With you, or with someone
else, Mr Grosse.

MAURICE. That's impossible and actually quite insulting.

PEGGY. If we are going to start shouting Mr Grosse you
know exactly where the door is...

MAURICE. Yes, yes, I'm sorry but Rey tomorrow, maybe
tomorrow, Mr Playfair can...

REY. He looks at me like I'm something the cat chucked
up. You know what he's like!

PEGGY. (*Powerful.*) No Rey, no. I've had enough of you
and your opinions. Talking about Mr Playfair like that,
when he's here night after night, helping us. Do you
hear me, Rey?

>   (**REY** *is rattled by* **PEGGY**'s *power.*)

MAURICE. *(Placating.)* He is the expert in these things, Rey. Really.

(Spider miaows again outside the window.)

REY. Right. Right you are.

(He looks at the gas fire. Shakes his head.)

Monkeys. They are monkeys them two.

(Calling.) Come along then Spider.

(And he goes. **MAURICE** *turn to* **PEGGY,** *smiles.)*

MAURICE. Well he's certainly a character.

PEGGY. A little too much talk for my taste, Mr Grosse.

MAURICE. Everyone needs a 'Rey' sometime. He's clearly very fond of you...

PEGGY. I've got quite enough on my plate. And you've seen him, the way he goes on?

MAURICE. He could keep you safe. From Eddie. I don't think even Eddie would want a run in with Rey. He'd talk him to death.

(He laughs at his own joke.)

PEGGY. Rey? He's lived in there listening to his own voice ever since his mother passed years ago. He's got a heart of gold I know, but no, Mr Grosse. *(She's smiling.)* I may be being driven crazy by all this, but *Rey!*

MAURICE. He could be a father to Jimmy. Jimmy needs someone, you know... If you don't mind me saying.

PEGGY. I think I should get myself to bed. *(Suddenly, she's fighting tears.)* I do mind you saying, as it happens. I can look after Jimmy. I know what he's 'like'. And the girls.

MAURICE. But they are frightened – you all are –

PEGGY. There's a soddin' poltergeist running havoc here!

MAURICE. That's not what I'm talking about.

PEGGY. I know what you are talking about.

MAURICE. I never meant...

PEGGY. When I was young Eddie wouldn't keep 'is hands off me. An' I'd do anything to keep him happy...

MAURICE. I was just trying to be practical – for the children.

PEGGY. I would turn heads before the babies, Mr Grosse, anyone'll tell you.

MAURICE. Oh I can imagine, but why don't we...

PEGGY. I didn't come from somewhere like you come from and I never had the chance to meet someone distinguished like you.

Truth be told, I wouldn't know what to do with someone like you, Mr Grosse. But Eddie? I knew what he was from the moment I clapped eyes on him but I couldn't, I wouldn't, turn away. And he had his way. And you shut your eyes and bobs your uncle, Mr Grosse, and I am here with three children who are a handful on their own, Rey popping over mornin', noon and night AND a poltergeist AND you two from the Society for Psychical Research or whatever the heck it's called.

(*Slight pause.*)

I'd like it all to have been different. But it's not. Some things you can't change.

MAURICE. We can all see the kind of woman you are.

PEGGY. Can you, really?

MAURICE. Of course! But why not *do* something... I'm sorry, that's not fair, but I...

PEGGY. Because my life isn't like that. And them girls' lives aren't going to be like that, an' Jimmy's isn't. What happens, happens *to* us. We are not like you.

> *(Slight pause.)*

We are ordinary. Eddie's just ordinary –

MAURICE. He's an animal.

PEGGY. *(Angry.)* You reckon you can see the kind of woman I am? You don't understand a thing. How can you? You have everything.

> *(There's an uneasy silence. Then* **PEGGY** *blushes – things have been said. Finally...)*

Hear how quiet it is now? This late?

> *(***MAURICE** *is still, listening, too, to the quiet.* **PEGGY** *turns and is about to go, but then she turns back. There is something resolved and intense about what she says next...)*

I feel sometimes it's like... well, that something *is* trapped here. In here. Something. Maybe someone.

(Change.) You are the experts. You shouldn't mind me.

(Changes – now a smile.) But something else: I do reckon we all *need* something. Something we can't understand.

> *(***PEGGY** *touches* **MAURICE** *on the arm.)*

I know you mean best.

> *(She turns and climbs the stairs. Finally,* **MAURICE** *is alone.)*

> *(He goes to the table. He looks at Janet's homework books. He looks up to the ceiling – waiting to hear* **PEGGY** *safely upstairs. Then he carefully opens the notebook. He turns the book – will another angle make sense? No.)*

*(Upstairs – **PEGGY** slips into bed.)*

*(Downstairs – **MAURICE** pulls on the headphones. He picks up his pencil to take notes and presses play. Again we hear the sound in his headphones in the theatre.)*

JANET ON TAPE. *(Her voice is weird and growly.)* GhhhghhhofuckoffIwantyouofhereoutof...

*(**MAURICE** winds the tape back.)*

GhhhghhhofuckoffIwantyouofhereoutof...

*(**MAURICE** stops the tape again. He changes the speed. This time **JANET**'s voice is deeper and weirder – but has a horrible clarity.)*

Ghhhhooooo FUCK OFF I WANT YOU OUT OF HERE... OUT OF MY FUCKING HOUSE... I CAN'T FUCKIN' SEE... I CAN'T FUCKING SEE... I want you...

*(**MAURICE** stops the tape. He looks around, fascinated. His mind is rushing. He looks up to the ceiling – it's quiet above.)*

*(Upstairs – **PEGGY** is finally drifting off to sleep. **JANET** is beside her in the double bed. Both **JIMMY** and **MARGARET** are sleeping on their beds.)*

*(Outside, the cat miaows again. **MAURICE** is more energised now.)*

(Somewhere in the distance, an ambulance siren whoops.)

*(**MAURICE** goes to the armchair and moves it downstage so that it faces the table with the tape recorder. He then takes out a microphone and puts it on a stand on the table.)*

MAURICE. *(Into the microphone.)* The black cat jumped over the moon...

> *(**MAURICE** puts the headphones on and presses play.)*

MAURICE ON TAPE. *(Echoing through the theatre.)* The black cat jumped over the moon...

> *(He takes off his headphones, satisfied. He now takes off his shoes, and turns towards the stairs when suddenly upstage a **GIRL** – it could be **MARGARET**, it could be **JANET** – floats two feet in the air. She is in an NHS hospital gown, her head is bandaged, and is moving towards **MAURICE**.)*

MAURICE. Janet?! Is that you Janet?!

> *(Then Spider miaows, **MAURICE** spins to see where the cat is. He turns back, the **GIRL** has disappeared.)*

Janet! Jan'! Jan'!

> *(Blackout.)*

Scene Four

(As **MAURICE**'s voice continues downstairs, upstairs **PEGGY** wakes and realises that **JANET** isn't beside her.)

PEGGY. Janet? Jan'?

(**PEGGY**'s movement triggers the flash bulbs.)

(Twisting, loud now.) Janet? Where's she gone? Jan'!

(FLASH as **MARGARET** sits up – frightened.)

MARGARET. Mum?

(FLASH as **PEGGY** pulls back the sheets.)

PEGGY. She's gone, she's not here!

(FLASH as **MARGARET** stands.)

MARGARET. (Calling.) Jan'! Janet!

PEGGY. Fetch Mr Grosse.

(**PEGGY** is trying to find her dressing gown [it is under the bedding she's just pulled back]. **MARGARET** runs to the stairs.)

(After her.) And put something decent on...

(More flashes as **JIMMY** sits up.)

JIMMY. Mum? What's happening?

PEGGY. (Clearly now very concerned.) It's alright Jimmy, it's alright.

(Downstairs – **MAURICE** is fast asleep on the sofa under his jacket. **MARGARET** spins into the room – she sees the stove in the middle of the room, turns to **MAURICE** –)

MARGARET. Mr Grosse, Mr Grosse…

>*(He doesn't stir – **MARGARET** is now alarmed.)*

Mr Grosse!

>*(Suddenly, he sits bolt upright.)*

MAURICE. Margaret, what are you doing *here*?!

MARGARET. *(Uneasy, laughing.)* It's our house – we live here Mr Grosse! Are you alright? Fuckin' 'ell!

PEGGY. *(Coming down the stairs.)* Jan' – she's not in the bed – she's gone. She's disappeared.

MAURICE. What do you mean? I…I saw her! She was here. Here!

>*(**MAURICE** is very unsettled – his shirt is untucked, his hair in chaos.)*

PEGGY. Janet, you in the toilet? You come out girl. She's in the toilet. Something happened to her…

>*(She goes towards the toilet –)*

(At the toilet door.) You in there Jan'?

MAURICE. No, she was here. I saw her, I saw her, there!

>*(He points where he saw the girl. He turns to where he heard the cat.)*

And the cat…

>*(**MAURICE** turns back and is now pointing towards **PEGGY** coming back from the toilet.)*

PEGGY. She's not here! She's not there.

MAURICE. *(Shouting, emotional.)* Listen to me. Something has happened – is happening – here! You got to hear me. I saw her. I saw Janet! I saw her!

(**JIMMY** *is on the stairs, he's terrified – seeing how distressed and excited* **MAURICE** *is.*)

JIMMY. It's alright, Mr Gr-r-osse...

PEGGY. You are frightening the boy! Will you stop this now?

MARGARET. *(Loud – shouting.)* Janet! Janet! You can stop playing around now.

MAURICE. I don't think she's playing around, I really don't.

MARGARET. *(Burying her desperation.)* But we all are. I told you Mr Grosse!

PEGGY. When did you see her? Where was she going?

MAURICE. Here. She was here.

(*He has run to where he saw the apparition.*)

JIMMY. Please mum...

(**JIMMY** *rushes downstairs and straight into* **PEGGY**'s *hug. This is all fast.*)

PEGGY. Mr Grosse, what did you see?

MAURICE. That she was here. Just here.

MARGARET. You didn't see nothing, Mr Grosse! I wanted to go to you-know-where, it was me...

PEGGY. *(Changing tack.)* Margaret, you run and fetch someone, please. But put something on!

MARGARET. *(To* **PEGGY**, *continuing.)* Mr Grosse was down there. Right there. *(She points at where* **MAURICE** *was.)* Staring at me. Like a right loon'. An' the cat was screeching...

MAURICE. *(Insistent, louder.)* It wasn't you Margaret! Don't you see. I wanted to talk to Janet and then she was there. *There. (He points, smiling excited.)* I saw her. Janet was alive there.

PEGGY. What do you mean alive? She's alive? What do you mean?

MARGARET. (*Insistent.*) We was playing around! Jan' and me!

> (*She stops because every fibre of energy in* **MAURICE** *has gone. He stops – looks at them all, then he stumbles to the sofa and sits. He realises he has been shouting and that he has lost it. He is appalled.*)

PEGGY. Mr Grosse – what are you talking about? What are you...

MAURICE. Oh, I am so sorry. Gosh. I don't know...

> (**MAURICE** *shudders,* **PEGGY** *turns to* **JIMMY** *and* **MARGARET**.)

PEGGY. Jimmy, boy, you stay here. Margaret, you put somethin' on an' fetch Uncle Rey. I'm going down the street.

MAURICE. (*Befuddled.*) What time is it? (*He looks at his watch.*) Three thirty in the morning – it's the most ghastly time of night. I'm so very sorry, children, I just, I don't know... something...

PEGGY. (*Interrupting, real strength.*) Just help me find Jan', Mr Grosse, please.

MAURICE. Yes, yes. (*He stands.*) But I think maybe I *should* go home. I'm sorry. So sorry.

JIMMY. No, you got t-t-t-o stay.

PEGGY. Just help me! Help us – please.

> (**PEGGY** *leaves* **JIMMY** *and goes towards the front door.*)

JIMMY. Mum.

PEGGY. It's alright. It's all going to be alright... Margaret, please...

MARGARET. *(Interrupting quieter – truthful.)* Jan's just messin' you around – you know that… we know that. I am too. Jimmy you know that. We are just messing!

PEGGY. But she's gone, she's gone. Janet's gone.

MAURICE. Where are my shoes, I'm sorry I shouldn't be here

MARGARET. *(Interrupting.)* It's not serious! It's not.

PEGGY. Please help me.

MARGARET. Mum.

PEGGY. Do as I say.

> *(But **MAURICE** kneels. Looks under the sofa.)*

MAURICE. *(Desperate.)* Where are my shoes? Oh where are my shoes? *(He finds them.)* Sorry, Peggy I can't…

> *(And then, upstage, the door rattles. Everyone freezes. It rattles again, more horrible now. Whatever energy has been building freezes. **PEGGY** hangs between determination and fear. **MAURICE** twists, vulnerable. **MARGARET** shivers.)*

JIMMY. Oh.

> *(The door rattles again.)*

MARGARET. *(Absolutely terrified.)* It's dad. He's drunk. It'll be bad. It's so late. Mum!

> *(She starts to weep. Terror. **PEGGY** holds out her arms.)*

PEGGY. Come here, girl.

> *(**MARGARET** crosses fast to **PEGGY**. **PEGGY** holds both **MARGARET** and **JIMMY**. The door rattles in its frame.)*

(Loud, shouting.) Eddie – get away from here!

(Nothing from outside.)

Get away. It's three in the morning! The children are asleep. Please.

(**MAURICE** *is still on his knees. There is another rattle.*)

MAURICE. *(Trying to be assertive.)* Hello. You should know I am here. You should know I will fetch the poli...

(But before he finishes, the door swings open. **REY** *stands holding* **JANET** *in his arms. Streetlight floods in behind them. She is in her nightie, deeply asleep.* **REY** *has the key in his hand – the rattling was him trying to get in the lock while holding* **JANET**.*)*

REY. She hasn't stirred or moved a muscle or nothing.

PEGGY. Jan'?! Where did you find her Rey? She alright? Jan' you alright?

(**MAURICE** *stands. We may now notice that* **PEGGY** *doesn't go to* **JANET** *– she's relieved but frightened.*)

MAURICE. We should put her down... is she cold?

PEGGY. Where was she, Rey?

MAURICE. Oh. She's very cold.

PEGGY. Rey?

(**REY** *gently puts* **JANET** *on the sofa.*)

REY. I woke up an' she was there.

PEGGY. What do you mean?

REY. Just felt something against me and I thought "What's that?" Didn't hear her breathing or anythin', amazing, really. She hasn't moved a muscle. Just stone cold like she's in a coma-thingy, you know.

REY. Jan' must have gone out for a walk, or somethin' and came in next door – got herself confused. It is four in the morning. Easy to get confused.

JIMMY. She-must-'ave gone th-rough the wall...

MARGARET. Maybe she was just sleep walkin'...

PEGGY. *(A strength we haven't seen before.)* Rey, I swear on everything that I hold sacred if you have anything to do with this, I will not rest...

*(**REY** turns to **PEGGY** startled.)*

REY. Me? I'm Uncle Rey?

MAURICE. Please, the child needs quiet.

PEGGY. If you...

MAURICE. *(Interrupting.)* Mrs Hodgson – I don't think...

PEGGY. *(To **MAURICE**.)* This is nothing to do with you.

REY. *(Mystified.)* Peggy, I didn't do nothing.

PEGGY. *(Exploding.)* Get out of my house! Get out of here! And don't ever think about coming back. You bastard...

REY. *(Deeply shocked.)* What are you talking about?

PEGGY. I seen you – the way you come here, every day. I thought you wanted to chat to me, but Margaret is right – you said, didn't you girl? How *Uncle* Rey looks at you? You get out of here, Rey –

REY. No, I never...

PEGGY. Get out of here.

> *(And she starts to beat on **REY**'s shoulder. It's violent and horrible. He takes blow after blow but starts to sob. Tears stream down his cheeks.)*

MARGARET. Mum...?

MAURICE. *(Over her.)* Peggy – please. He didn't take Janet...

PEGGY. This has got nothing to do with you Mr Grosse. Nothing.

>*(She pulls away from **REY**. Then roars –)*

I want you *all* to go. *All* of you.

>*(She points at the table – the tape recorder, the microphone.)*

Get all of that out of here. Now. And Rey how *dare* you. Look at her – she's no more than skin and bones.

REY. I never...

MAURICE. *(At the same time.)* Please, Peggy, things are... I'm sure what Rey... Mr Playfair says things...

>*(Then **MARGARET** screams –)*

MARGARET. He's there!

>*(As she points up the stairs we get a glimpse of the **MAN**, on his crutch, staring down at her.)*

He's upstairs!

>*(The others spin and look, but the **MAN** has gone. **MARGARET** runs to **PEGGY**, she's shivering and shuddering.)*

Mum, mum there's a man upstairs. A man.

>*(**MARGARET**, **PEGGY** and **JIMMY** are all hugging each other when...)*

JIMMY. Mum...

PEGGY. It's alright.

>*(A pool of urine forms around **JIMMY**'s feet. His pyjamas are soaked.)*

PEGGY. *(Quietly.)* OK, boy, OK.

REY. I... Peggy, you have to believe me – I just woke up – she was there. I didn't do nothing. I wouldn't want any harm to Jan' or any of you. She's just a child.

MARGARET. Please mum. Please I'm frightened. He's upstairs – there's a man upstairs.

REY. You want me to go up, Peggy? I'm not having this. I am not having this.

> *(But he doesn't move. Then **REY** has a new idea.)*

Listen, come next door. You will be safe there. Nothing ever happens next door.

PEGGY. I'm not leaving here. I'm not leaving this house.

MAURICE. You all... we all have to get some sleep. It'll be morning soon.

REY. Peggy, please, we should get the children to bed, at least. I'll stay in the lounge. You have the upstairs.

PEGGY. I'm not leaving Jan'. Jan' Jan', wake up.

> *(But **JANET** doesn't wake.)*

I'm going to fetch something, I'm going to fetch an ambulance... Please.

> *(**MAURICE** goes to **JANET**. Kneels in front of her. Takes her pulse.)*

MAURICE. She's alright, I promise you. I will keep watch. This has been going on for three months now. The child is simply exhausted. Let her sleep. I'm just going to sit here.

> *(He points at a chair, and sits on it.)*

REY. Might be for the best. A couple of hours sleep.

(Whispers to **PEGGY**.*)* Sort out the poor lad, also. Get him dry?

JIMMY. I'm sorry Mr Grosse, I-I-I didn't mean to...

MAURICE. That's alright Lieutenant Hodgson. Happened to better men.

> (**MAURICE** *picks up the pyjamas that* **PEGGY** *was repairing at the beginning.*)

Please. No one can go on like this. Everyone will be safe with you at Rey's house.

REY. That's right, Peg'. Safe as houses there.

MARGARET. Please mum – I'm frightened.

> (**PEGGY** *crosses to* **JANET**, *takes her hand, strokes her head.*)

PEGGY. Mr Grosse?

> *(He nods – affirmative.)*

(Whispering.) She's asleep. That's good.

MAURICE. Leave her with me. She can sleep. And she's warming up now. You go to next door. You get some rest. *(He smiles.)* Everything will look very different in the daylight.

> *(Spider miaows outside the kitchen window.)*

(Half laughing.) And you can do us a favour and take that poor benighted cat with you!

(Very gentle.) Put these... *(The pyjamas.)* ...on the boy. If anything happens I will know where you are. Honestly, I will. Please Peggy, it's for the best.

> (**PEGGY** *nods.*)

REY. You come to my house. It's alright there.

PEGGY. Cummon, Jimmy, let's...

> (*And she leads him upstage into the kitchen.*
> **REY**, **MARGARET** *and* **MAURICE** *stand –*
> *uneasily.*)

REY. (*He grins, whispers.*) Gets into people's heads, don't it?

MAURICE. Yes.

> (*There's a pause.*)

It is going to be quite a thing to describe to Mr Playfair and the other investigators. Quite a night.

MARGARET. I thought you were takin' the night off. I thought that's what you said?

> (**MAURICE** *smiles – embarrassed, caught out.*)

MAURICE. Probably better if we keep shtum and say nothing to Mr Playfair.

> (*Slight pause.* **REY** *points at the tape recorder.*)

REY. But you getting good stuff – with the cameras and the whattisname?

MAURICE. Heavens yes. Extraordinary, actually. The science of all this is quite something. I think the goings on here will be in the history books.

> (**PEGGY** *and* **JIMMY** *reappear.* **MAURICE**
> *smiles.*)

Shipshape and ready, young Jimmy? You need some sleep. All of you. There will be hell to pay if you children go to school with match-sticks in your eyes. Isn't that right?

> (**REY** *leads away.*)

PEGGY. I'll be back in an hour –

MAURICE. Try and get some sleep.

PEGGY. I don't think I'll ever sleep again.

(*She follows* **REY** *and* **JIMMY** *out the back door.* **MARGARET** *stops and turns – looks at* **MAURICE**.)

MAURICE. Get some sleep young woman. Get some sleep.

MARGARET. What do you want from Jan'?

(**MAURICE** *blinks, then smiles.*)

MAURICE. No more of your games young lady.

(**MARGARET** *laughs.*)

MARGARET. Not a game, is it, Mr Grosse?

(*She turns and goes. The back door closes. Finally, alone,* **MAURICE** *sits on the chair near the tape recorder. He then stands and turns off almost all of the lights. Finally, he turns towards* **JANET** *and looks down on her.*)

(*He glances back at the door. No one has had second thought, they are safely alone.* **MAURICE** *then kneels beside* **JANET**. *He then decides and puts his arms around her and drags – carries –* **JANET** *to the armchair. It's like he is dancing with a corpse.*)

(*Finally,* **MAURICE** *shuffles her into the chair and pulls back, breathing hard.*)

MAURICE. There – there. My love.

(*He then goes carefully through to the front door, opens it, and goes out. For a moment,* **JANET** *is alone. The lights hold on her. We watch her; she stirs, looks around. Hearing* **MAURICE** *returning, she slumps back.* **MAURICE** *comes back carrying a car rug that he wraps around* **JANET**.)

MAURICE. Your daddy rug.

(Quietly.) You know, dear, when the telephone started to ring, I was actually having a little snooze. It had been the most perfect day. We'd played some golf and had a bit of lunch with Derek and Isabel. Do you remember them? As soon as I heard the telephone – your mother answered – I could tell something terrible had happened. I could tell from Mummy's voice.

> *(He looks at her, thinks, continues.)*

I knew straight away that things weren't going to be the same again.

I felt the same thing when Granny died. But this was different. Mummy kept saying: "But we are in Jersey. We are on holiday in Jersey." As though that would make the slightest bit of difference. So I took charge. They told me that at about three thirty in the morning, there'd been an accident. Involving a motorbike. I had to take charge.

First plane the next morning, and we were on it. Then we drove. Drove and drove. Mummy was shivering and I wrapped her in your 'daddy rug' from the car.

> *(Slight pause.)*

It was six in the evening when we got to Cardiff.

(This is tough.) We went into the Casualty Department. Horrible place. I was walking and even though it was still hot – it had been a very hot day – Jan', I was shivering, too. Can you hear me dearest?

(He's weeping.) But no one knew where you were. Can you imagine that? After that drive, after everything we were going through? So I asked a nurse: "I'm so sorry but don't you know where my daughter is? She was involved in an accident last night. On a motorcycle." I needed to be with you, Janet. I knew we could help you.

But the nurse at the desk didn't have her brain plugged in at all and I, and Mummy, we just started shouting for you. Calling out loud. We made quite a scene. And then a Sister came and said, no name, no pack drill, – "Janet Grosse has cracked her skull. Her injuries are..."

(He shrugs this away.)

She then marched us through the hospital. First this way, then that. We passed someone serving tea, two nurses laughing about what had happened at the weekend, I suppose, and then...

*(**MAURICE** holds **JANET**'s hands now, pulling her to him.)*

The sun was still baking. Outside across some buildings, some lads were playing cricket. Everything felt so normal.

(He gasps – this is unbearable.)

Your head was bandaged, wrapped... they'd shaved your hair, your beautiful hair, and all I could hear was... all I could hear was the machines...

(Absolutely now in the present.) Janet, Janet. We are here. Mummy and Daddy. We are here. It's all OK. Tell us you can hear us...

*(Suddenly **JANET**'s eyes open. **MAURICE** freezes.)*

JANET. Daddy –

(Her voice is clear – middle class.)

MAURICE. Janet?

JANET. What on earth are you doing here, Daddy?

MAURICE. You were involved in an accident. On Eric's motorbike, Janet, my darling. Mummy and Daddy came as soon as we could.

JANET. Mummy?

MAURICE. Yes, darling. Yes we came as soon as we heard. Your mother is very distressed. You are going to be OK, they have done a little op'... we are here Janet...

JANET. *(Interrupting.)* Mummy... Where's Mummy?

MAURICE. Everything is alright. Tell me you are alright...

JANET. I'm alright, Daddy. I'm super, actually. Everyone is so kind to me. They are so very kind.

MAURICE. Oh that's marvellous. Yes that's marvellous.

JANET. Oh yes, Daddy. Granny is here, also. I think.

MAURICE. *(Taken aback.)* My mother? Oh. Gosh.

JANET. Everyone is here – soldiers too, Daddy, like the fellas you knew from the war, yes? Achtung! Stuka soldiers. They are all here.

MAURICE. *(Now confused.)* With you? From the beach? They are *with* you?

JANET. When are you coming, dear Daddy? When will we all be together?

MAURICE. Coming?

(Now he understands.)

In time, my darling, in my time.

JANET. Oh that's good Daddy.

MAURICE. I love you Janet. We all love you so much. Everyone loves you...

JANET. That's good. That's very good. That's super, Daddy, dear. I want to see Mummy, too.

*(**JANET** becomes quieter and closes her eyes. As the lights fade and sound – a memory takes over. A child's voice singing a nursery rhyme leads as the lights change.)*

Scene Five

(Birdsong.)

CHILD JANET VOICE. Jack and Jill went up the hill To fetch a pail of water. Jack fell down and broke his crown, And Jill came tumbling after.

*(A voice rings out – it is **BETTY**, Maurice's wife.)*

BETTY'S VOICE. *(Happy.)* You'd better come in now. Time to stop playing, children, it's time for tea.

*(The first light of dawn, an urban dawn chorus. **MAURICE** is fast asleep on the sofa. As the light grows, we realise the gas stove is back in place. **JANET** has gone. The rug is neatly folded on a chair.)*

MAURICE'S VOICE. *(Happy, loving.)* Look at that, my darling. Look at that. We will always remember this sunny afternoon. We will remember this sunny afternoon all our lives.

BETTY'S VOICE. *(Calling, easy.)* Children, come in now...

*(The sound of a car. A car door closes. Feet outside and then, for the first time, the doorbell rings. **MAURICE** doesn't wake. The doorbell rings again, maybe a third time. Then, after a moment, a figure appears upstage, looking in the kitchen window. Then, the back door rattles. **MAURICE** now sits up. He turns and goes to the kitchen door – still half asleep. The figure is **BETTY**, Maurice's wife. She is dressed in a twin set and pearls but shattered by grief. Dislocated by grief.)*

MAURICE. *(Surprised.)* Betty?

BETTY. Maurice. Mr Playfair turned up at the house. You know I don't like him. He was surprised you weren't in – he wanted to introduce you to some Brazilians. They were ghastly, really weird. They looked at me like a hangman might.

> *(She shudders at the thought, and walks into the house. She stares around.)*

It's smaller than I imagined.

> *(She looks at **MAURICE**.)*

I lied for you Maurice. I said that you were out. With friends. We don't have friends, now though, do we?

MAURICE. I had to be here. The children's father comes on a Wednesday. He pretends he still lives here. Claims his social. He's a monster. He terrifies them…

> *(But **MAURICE** is distracted – he goes to the gas fire. Looks at it. Turns, mystified.)*

BETTY. That's our car rug.

(Swallowing emotion.) That is Janet's rug, Maurice. What is it doing here?

> *(**MAURICE** looks at the rug, confused.)*

She used to love her 'daddy rug'.

> *(**MAURICE** turns to **BETTY**.)*

MAURICE. I was right. I am right. No, listen to me – I… The girl here is being used, that's clear. I know what you feel about him but Mr Playfair really can explain. There are 'others', on the other side, trapped. Janet was trying to get to me through her. Through a portal. I'm sure. I'm certain of it Betty.

I spoke with her. You were here with me.

BETTY. What are you talking about?

> (**MAURICE**'s *hand goes to his mouth – his emotions totally overwhelm him for a second.*)

MAURICE. *(Starting to sob.)* She's alright! Betty, she's not alone. Janet's not alone. She's alright. She's with my mother!

BETTY. *(Real power.)* This is nonsense. It is disgusting nonsense, Maurice. Cruel nonsense. Janet is gone. We buried Janet. She died. Eric lost control of that bloody bike. The roads were like ice after the heat. You know that.

MAURICE. But I was with her. Betty, dear, we were with her. Here.

> (**PEGGY** *is on the stairs, unnoticed by either* **BETTY** *or* **MAURICE**.)

BETTY. You've gone mad – those people. Those fucking Brazilians. Mr Playfair. They are all freaks...

MAURICE. We have tapes, and photographs Betty! I hate mumbo jumbo, you know that. I am a practical man...

> *(Slight pause.)*

And don't you see, Betty, darling? She is called *Janet* too! I was so, so lucky. We are so lucky. Don't you see...?

> (**BETTY** *takes* **MAURICE**'s *hands.*)

BETTY. You must come home now. You've lost your mind, Maurice. To think...

MAURICE. No she'll... I'm sure...she's here.

PEGGY. Mrs Grosse?

BETTY. *(Turning, startled.)* Yes?

PEGGY. I wondered how long you could do without him. I heard the doorbell.

*(**PEGGY** walks down the stairs and passes **BETTY**.)*

BETTY.　Oh I'm sorry –

MAURICE.　This family, this house, Betty, they've been through such terrible things!

*(**PEGGY** faces **MAURICE**.)*

PEGGY.　You pull yourself together Mr Grosse, can you? I got to get my nippers something to eat before they go to school and don't want them to see you in a state, like this.

MAURICE.　Who moved the gas fire, Mrs Hodgson?

PEGGY.　Put your shoes, and your jacket, on.

MAURICE.　Did Rey bring some lads over while I was asleep?

PEGGY.　An' here... give that a bit of a blow.

> *(She hands him a hanky – he blows his tears away. **PEGGY** continues into the kitchen.)*

(Calling back.) A cup of tea, Mrs Grosse, to set you on your way...

MAURICE.　*(This will prove it.)* I'm afraid our friend smashed your...

> *(**PEGGY** has the teapot. She puts the kettle on. **MAURICE** stares.)*

PEGGY.　*(Over shoulder.)* Come far Mrs Grosse?

BETTY.　Wimbledon. Maurice...

> *(**PEGGY** brings a box of Weetabix to the table –)*

MAURICE.　What about Eddie? What will you do if he comes around?

PEGGY. *(Calling upstairs – singing the advert.)* "Pullback the sheetsabix...

(To **BETTY**, *smiling.)* No wonder Weetabix is unbeatbix..."

(She turns to **MAURICE** *– and is clear and firm.)*

I can handle my husband, Mr Grosse.

*(***JANET** *comes down the stairs in her school uniform. She looks more strained than ever...)*

MAURICE. Oh there she is!

(Change.) Janet, dearest.

PEGGY. *(Calling, over.)* Now where's that lad of mine Jimmy...?

MAURICE. This is my wife Betty. Betty Grosse. Mrs Grosse.

*(***JANET** *stops. She stares at* **BETTY**.*)*

JANET. Yes, yes, I know.

*(***JANET** *picks up the car rug and wraps it around her shoulders...)*

BETTY. What's she doing?

(Growing fear.) That doesn't belong to you, young lady.

JANET. *(In her posh voice – but absolutely serious.)* Oh gosh but I have known you since I was a baby, haven't I? I saw you first, didn't I?

BETTY. Maurice?! What's she doing?

*(***JANET** *embraces* **BETTY**, *wrapping her in the car rug.)*

JANET. Mummy. Oh Mummy, hold me.

BETTY. *(Frightened.)* Maurice?

JANET. Did you come? Did you come from Jersey?

PEGGY. Jan', I want you to stop this.

BETTY. *(Sobbing.)* Maurice – Maurice who is she? Janet?

> *(**JANET** holds **BETTY** firmly.)*

PEGGY. Jan'.

JANET. Oh Mummy. Oh Mummy.

PEGGY. Janet!

BETTY. Who are you, child? Who are you?

MAURICE. Can't you see?

> *(**BETTY** tries to get out of **JANET**'s embrace.*
> *She's squirming, but **JANET**'s embrace is*
> *tightening.)*

BETTY. Please, God...

JANET. Mummy oh Mummy.

BETTY. Let go of me!

MAURICE. It's Janet, darling, it's Janet!

> *(**PEGGY** is watching, **MARGARET** has stopped*
> *on the stairs. Both **PEGGY** and **MARGARET***
> *watch – this is getting horrible. **BETTY** is*
> *gasping as **JANET** hangs onto her.)*

BETTY. No! No! Please, no. Janet, no.

PEGGY. *(Powerful.)* Stop now Jan'! Do as I say.

> *(**JANET** suddenly breaks from **BETTY** and*
> *slumps onto a chair. She looks tiny and*
> *fragile. Her whole body is exhausted. Then*
> *she pulls whatever energy she has together*
> *and...)*

JANET. Better get ready for school, or there'll be 'ell to pay.
What's for brekkie?

(MARGARET goes fast to JANET and puts her hand on her shoulder.)

(Hissing at her like a cat.) Don't want to touch what is not yours, do you?

(MARGARET steps back, frightened.)

MARGARET. Jan'?

PEGGY. *(Making bright.)* Cummon you ragamuffins we got company! Weetabix...

(She goes back to her kitchen. Just for a moment PEGGY seems frozen, even horrified.)

MARGARET. *(Picking up PEGGY's tone.)* Eatabix! Greetabix!

BETTY. Maurice – she's burnt me. She's burnt my hands.

(She holds up her hands. The flesh is red and burnt. PEGGY comes out of the kitchen carrying the full teapot, she has recovered.)

PEGGY. *(Bright.)* That cuppa, Mrs Grosse? But maybe you want to get on your way or you'll be snarled up the morning rush, I expect, Mr Grosse?

(JANET starts to growl.)

JANET. IWANT YOU TO FUCKOFFI WANT YOU TO GO...

(BETTY reaches for MAURICE – her hand is shaking.)

BETTY. Maurice, please.

PEGGY. Mrs Grosse? A cup of tea?

JANET. GOTOFUCKANBURNINFUCKINGHELL.

BETTY. *(Barely able to speak.)* Kind of you, no. No thank you.

JANET. GRRRR – GRRR – PISSNSHIT...

PEGGY. Shouldn't pay too much attention to the children, should she, Mr Grosse? It's all a bit of fun, Mrs Grosse.

MAURICE. Mrs Hodgson...?

BETTY. *(Whispering.)* Maurice, is that girl Janet?

> (**MAURICE** *breaks from* **BETTY** *and grabs Janet's school book.* **JANET** *is growling...)*

MAURICE. *(To* **PEGGY**.*)* What's this then?

> *(But he's leafing through the exercise books and frowns. Wonders if he's opened the book the wrong way.)*

(Calling to **JANET**.*)* Have you been writing here? What is this?

> (**JANET** *stops growling.)*

This is a nursery rhyme, Janet? Look, this is something *we* sang, Betty, dear lo...

> (**JANET** *moves like lightning – grabs the school book.)*

JANET. Mine!

(She turns, hissing.) Private. Mine. Leave it.

MAURICE. But when did you write this...?

JANET. No-one likes a nosey-parker!

> (**JIMMY** *is coming down the stairs now, loud and full of energy.)*

JIMMY. Mr G-rosse, c-an y-ou t-ell us about how y-ou were attacked by that St-uka again at the beach? T-onight.

BETTY. Maurice I am leaving. I am going.

JIMMY. P-p-lease, Mr Grosse?

*(**BETTY** pulls at **MAURICE**'s hand.)*

BETTY. Maurice, I don't want to be here.

PEGGY. Eat your brekkie, Jimmy, there'll be lots of time to ask Mr Grosse about everything...

> *(**JANET**, **MARGARET**, **JIMMY** now sit at the table. **MARGARET** and **JIMMY** eat their breakfast. **JANET** is now still. **PEGGY** pours herself a cup of tea.)*

PEGGY. That's better.

BETTY. *(Absolute.)* We have to go, Maurice. We shouldn't be here.

MAURICE. Peggy? Janet?

> *(They don't look at him.)*

(Plaintiff.) Lieutenant Hodgson?

> *(**JIMMY** shuffles his food, glances up, and then back to his bowl.)*

MARGARET. He's a very naughty boy is your Mr Grosse, Mrs Gro...

> *(A look from **PEGGY** silences her as **BETTY** pulls at **MAURICE**.)*

BETTY. Please, Maurice, what is this? Please...

> *(**MAURICE** breaks from **BETTY**. He squats beside **JANET**. The family appear now, not even to see him.)*

MAURICE. Janet, tell me what has happened. What is going on?

PEGGY. *(To the **CHILDREN**.)* Who's lookin' forward to a lovely day? Nippers?

BETTY. I'm going...

>*(Distressed, she turns and runs towards the door and out.* **MARGARET** *starts to whisper the lyrics of the Bay City Rollers' "I Only Want to Be with You". While* **MAURICE** *tries to get through to any of them.)*

MAURICE. It *is* scientific, what Mr Playfair and I do...

>*(***PEGGY*** *now joins the* **GIRLS** *singing.)*

Please, tell me what...

>*(Nothing.* **MAURICE** *turns, and then turns back.)*

Probably best if Mr Playfair didn't...

>*(No one responds.* **MAURICE** *goes out the front door. Finally, the sound of a car starting. Driving away. Pause.)*

JIMMY. I-I-I-hope Mr Grosse c-comes tonight.

>*(***PEGGY*** *pours herself another cup of tea, stirs three sugars in. Carefully drinks her tea.)*

PEGGY. That's better.

MARGARET.   Dad'll be here tonight. He didn't come yesterday. He'll be here tonight.

>*(***PEGGY*** *sips her tea.)*

JIMMY. Y-You should m-marry Mr Grosse mum, he'd see Dad off...

MARGARET. Mr Grosse is already married, you fucking spaz'.

JIMMY. Or Rey t-then. He could keep us s-s-safe.

>*(***JANET*** *suddenly stands.)*

JANET. No he can't. None of them can. No one can.

(*Then absolutely clear.*) No one can keep you safe.

(*And she turns and goes out the door.*)

PEGGY. Jan'! Go after her –

JIMMY. (*Shouting.*) Jan' wait…!

(**JIMMY** *follows fast.*)

PEGGY. (*Calling after them.*) Use the zebra crossing, Jimmy!

(**JIMMY**'s *gone.*)

MARGARET. I don't want to be like this no more, Mum. I don't.

PEGGY. (*Gently.*) It will be alright. It will, it will.

MARGARET. You know what we did?

PEGGY. You didn't do nothing, Maggie. You are good children. The best.

MARGARET. I better catch up with them. Jan' will just step out in front of a bus if I'm not there…

PEGGY. (*Calling.*) And you behave yourself, young lady. Behave.

(**MARGARET** *is gone. Finally, the door slams shut and* **PEGGY** *is alone. She starts to clear the breakfast and humming the Bay City Rollers when, from the kitchen window, a loud miaow.*)

(*Indulgent.*) I wondered where you'd got to Spider.

(*Another miaow and* **PEGGY** *notices that* **JANET** *has left the school books and her satchel.*)

Oh Jan' you silly sausage.

(**PEGGY** *picks up the bag and books and runs out the door.*)

(*Blackout.*)

(*Distant* **CHILDREN** *singing:*)

CHILDREN. *(Singing.)* Jack fell down and broke his crown, And Jill came tumbling after.

(*And suddenly the* **MAN** *is sitting in the armchair in the centre of the room.*)

(*He's clearer now. His leg has recently been amputated, urine dribbles out of a catheter, his hands grasp the chair and he is roaring louder and louder. What he says is mostly incomprehensible as screams and howling. Blind. Then a chair flips. Then the doors upstairs slam repeatedly. He points at the gas fire. Boof – flames leap out of the fire. The table shakes. Smoke seems to be consuming the* **MAN***, but he is talking to all of us.*)

MAN.   FUCKOFFSHITHOLEI WANTYOUOUTOF HERE... OUTOFMYFUCKING HOUSE... I want you... OUT OF MY HOUSE.

(*Blackout.*)

CHILDREN. *(Singing, distant.)* Jack and Jill went up the hill To fetch a pail of water. Jack fell down and broke his crown, And Jill came tumbling after.

(*And in the darkness – the* **CHILDREN** *sing – quietly, scarily and the cat miaows around the audience, behind them. And then under seat J28...*)

The End

Milton Keynes UK
Ingram Content Group UK Ltd.
UKHW021831171123
432775UK00012B/650